Radical Prayer

9 Biblical Concepts That Will Forever Change the Way You Pray

Monte Kline

Published by:

Pacific Health Center
PO Box 857
Sahuarita, AZ 85629
www.pacifichealthcenter.com

ISBN-13: 978-1546686606
ISBN-10: 1546686606

Copyright 2017 by Monte L. Kline

All Rights Reserved. No part of this book may be reproduced or transmitted in any form or by any means, electronic or mechanical, including photocopy, recording, or by an information storage and retrieval system – except by a reviewer who may quote brief passages in a review to be printed in a magazine or newspaper or online – without permission in writing from the publisher.

All Bible references are from *The Holy Bible, English Standard Version*, copyright 2000, 2001 by Crossway Bibles, a division of Good News Publishers, 1300 Crescent Street, Wheaton, IL 60187, USA.

Table of Contents

Introduction

Chapter 1 – Concept #1 – Radical Purpose

Chapter 2 – Concept #2 – Radical Decree

Chapter 3 – Concept #3 – Radical Will

Chapter 4 – Concept #4 – Radical Praise

Chapter 5 – Concept #5 – Radical Meditation

Chapter 6 – Concept #6 – Radical Confession

Chapter 7 – Concept #7 – Radical Petition

Chapter 8 – Concept #8 – Radical Order & Argument

Chapter 9 – Concept #9 – Radical Intercession

Chapter 10 – Radical Psalms

Chapter 11 – Radical Examples – Hannah, Daniel & Paul

Chapter 12 – Radical Model – The "Lord's Prayer"

Chapter 13 – Radical Relationship – The Real Lord's Prayer

Closing Thoughts

About the Author

Appendix A – Prayer Applied: Encounter God through Personal Retreats

Appendix B – Discover Health in Body, Mind & Spirit

Introduction

I would rather teach one man to pray than ten men to preach.
— Charles Spurgeon

What is "radical" prayer? While the word "radical" may suggest to some a political insurrection, the word is actually defined as:

1. From the roots; going to the foundation of something
2. A favoring of fundamental or extreme change

I became convinced I needed to go to the root of prayer and make a fundamental change in my prayer life. I have observed that most Christians occupy that same position. Thus, this is a book of radical concepts on prayer – not radical as compared to the Bible, but radical compared to contemporary Christian practice.

I needed **radical prayer,** and you probably do to, for there is more misunderstanding per square inch about prayer than about any subject I know of! As a young Christian during college, I was no exception. I wanted to grow into a spiritual giant and knew that prayer was apparently the key – at least according to all the biographies of great Christians. I wanted to discover the method – the formula – for super-spirituality. For example I read Martin Luther's quote:

> *If I fail to spend two hours in prayer each morning, the devil gets the victory through the day. I have so much business I cannot get on without spending three hours daily in prayer.*

Wow! Maybe I need to spend two or three hours in prayer before I start my day. I decided to try that. I was working a maintenance job painting Crater Lake Lodge in Crater Lake National Park in Oregon that summer and had access to the small paint storage room in the basement of the lodge. So at 4 AM I would go down to the basement, unlock that door and pray amidst the paint cans – at least until my boss noted my presence one early morning and suggested there were better places to pray!

Like many new (and old) Christians, I was very "works" oriented, falsely believing that I could **do** some spiritual discipline and become a spiritual giant. Fortunately grace eventually won out, teaching me that spirituality was a matter of heart-change, rather than mere effort in spiritual activities.

Survey about any group of Christians asking, "What is the most important thing you can do in the Christian life," and I suspect most will answer as Pastor Chuck Smith did:

> *The most important thing a born again Christian can do is to pray.*

Theologian Joel Beeke said:

> *Prayer is the thermometer of our spiritual life, the breath of our soul.*[1]

Martin Luther was even more emphatic:

> *To be a Christian without prayer is no more possible than to be alive without breathing.*

We instinctively and intuitively believe in the supremacy of prayer, whether from reading Scripture itself, from reading biographies of great Christians who invariably were great men and women of prayer or perhaps just from the inner leading of the Holy Spirit. Prayer is supremely important, but do we know how to actually pray? Unfortunately, most of us do not – and this isn't a new problem.

The **only** thing the disciples ever asked Jesus to teach them was how to pray (Luke 11:1). Think about that. They didn't ask him to teach them to preach, to teach, to study Scripture, to counsel, to evangelize or any other "ministry" activity, but to pray . . . and make no mistake, we must be "taught" to pray – it won't come naturally. They obviously sensed the importance of prayer, particularly as they were awed by the example of Jesus. I might add that you will look long and hard in the curriculum of any theological seminary to find a course teaching future pastors how to pray. How could they miss the most important thing?

PRAYER PARADOX

While Christians would agree that prayer is so very important, paradoxically most would honestly say they either don't pray enough and/or they are disappointed in the quality of their prayer life. So, how can it be that we all feel prayer is so important, and yet we stink at it? Could it be we never really learned how to correctly pray?

A few years ago I suddenly realized that my prayers bore scant resemblance to the prayers in the Bible. I wasn't praying *biblically*. So how was I praying? Probably the same way you are praying, following the examples of other Christians at church and elsewhere I've been around over the years – other Christians who likewise didn't know how to pray biblically. The blind have been leading the blind. You see, prayer can be a very demotivating activity, **if** you don't do it correctly. On the other hand, when you learn to pray biblically, like David or Daniel or Jeremiah or Paul or Peter or Jesus, prayer actually gets exciting **because you see results**.

This book was borne out of my frustration with a lousy prayer life in desperate need of radical change. In my life that change has begun to be something beautiful and exciting – and I emphasize "begun," because I feel my paltry insights are barely scratching the surface. I can say that, even at my "baby step" level, my prayer life has been transformed. It is my prayer that you too will experience a radical change in your prayer life. Let's begin!

FOOTNOTES:

1. Beeke, Joel R., *Revelation*, (Grand Rapids: Reformation Heritage Books, 2016), p. 252.

Chapter 1

Radical Purpose

Prayer now feels less about asking for something and more about enjoying someone. – Larry Crabb

What exactly is the purpose of prayer? Why do we pray? Are we praying about the right things? You'll never pray correctly and effectively until you radically alter your understanding of the **purpose** of prayer – a purpose I am convinced that most Christians do not grasp.

One of the greatest insights I've ever come across on prayer (and rebukes to my own prayer life) comes from a story Dr. Larry Crabb shares in his book The PAPA Prayer:

> *I picked up a good friend this morning at eleven o'clock. We were going to run a few errands and then grab some lunch. I invited him along because I wanted to be with him. I like his company. I told him I was writing a book on prayer. "What's your big idea?" he asked. "Well, as I've always said, prayer is the weakest part of my Christian life. I've read stories about great men of prayer, like George Muller, and wondering what I was doing wrong. It's just recently become clear to me that my prayer life has been mostly about trying to get God to do something for me. That never seemed wrong before." He was still listening, so I continued. "I've read books that say prayer is an opportunity to have a conversation with God, like two good friends getting to know each other better. And that never made sense to me. But it does now. . . Prayer now feels less about asking for something and more about enjoying someone. As I get to know God better and learn to trust His good intentions toward me, what I desire most falls more into line with what He desires, and I end up asking for what I know we both want."*
>
> *My friend turned toward me and said, "Suppose when you picked me up, the first thing I said to you had been, 'Larry, I need you to come by*

our house tonight. Mary and I need your advice about something. And could you run by the drugstore? I need to pick up a prescription.' When we sit down for lunch, I ask you about one of my kids. 'And oh, by the way, any chance of a loan? Things have been pretty tight. To be honest with you, I'm hoping you'll pick up lunch, if that's OK.'" He continued, "How would you feel if I talked to you like that? Yet that's how I talk to God. As you were telling me about your book, that just popped into my mind. I'd never do that to you. I like just being with you. But I don't know how to just be with God. So I ask Him for lots of things."[1]

Do you know how to just "be" with God, or do you just ask him for "stuff?" George McDonald put it this way:

But if God is so good as you represent Him, and if He knows all that we need, and better far than we do ourselves, why should it be necessary to ask Him for anything? I answer, What if He knows prayer to be the thing we need first and most? What if the main object in God's idea of prayer be the supplying of our great, our endless need — the need of Himself? Hunger may drive the runaway child home, and he may or may not be fed at once, but he needs his mother more than his dinner. Communion with God is the one need of the soul beyond all other needs: prayer is the beginning of that communion, and some need is the motive of that prayer. So begins a communion, a talking with God, a coming-to-one with Him, which is the sole end of prayer.

Pastor Tim Keller remarks:

. . . ordinarily our prayers are not varied — they consist usually of petitions, occasionally some confession (if we have just done something wrong). Seldom or never do we spend sustained time adoring and praising God. In short, we have no positive, inner desire to pray. We do it only when circumstances force us. Why? We know God is there, but we tend to see him as a means through which we get things to make us happy. For most of us, he has not become our happiness. We therefore pray to procure things, not to know him better.[2]

How about your prayer life? Is just "being" with God,

communing with him, talking to him and ultimately coming to oneness with him your primary purpose in prayer? If not, it's time for a radical change. But first, let's dig into this concept a little deeper.

TAKE INVENTORY

What is your greatest deficiency in prayer?

>   Lack motivation to pray?
>   Lack results from praying?
>   Don't know what to pray?
>   Prayer just feels awkward?

When you pray, what's your primary concern?

>   Getting something from God?
>   Thanking God for something he has given?
>   Spending time with God (communion)?
>   Seeking God's glory?
>   Worshipping God?

If you're stuck on prayer just being the way you try to get stuff from God, like a child begging a parent to buy them a piece of candy, you are guaranteed to have an inferior, unfulfilling prayer life. By contrast prayer that focuses not on "getting stuff," but rather on being in the presence of God is amazing. This kind of a prayer life will primarily be characterized, not by speaking so much as by listening.

LISTEN UP!

> *Be still and know that I am God* (Psalm 46:10a)

That's a polite way of saying, "You need to shut up more when you pray." There's far too much talking in our prayer and not enough listening. A conversation, including a conversation with God, involves both talking and listening. Andrew Murray wrote:

> *Take time. Give God time to reveal Himself to you. Give yourself time*

to be silent and quiet before Him, waiting to receive, through the Spirit, the assurance of His presence with you, His power working in you.

I remember one particular client in my years of clinical practice that provided the most wonderful *negative* example of this. During her entire appointment she absolutely would not stop talking, going from one topic to another. I honestly don't know when she found time to breathe! Normally, as I am performing our computerized, non-invasive nutritional testing, I provide a running commentary of the tests and their results. Of course I talk because I know what's going on. I know the interpretation of the test results. My clients don't know that, so they usually mostly listen with an occasional clarifying question.

So what did I do? I just let her talk while I continued the testing. Though it was very annoying, I got the test results I needed. The problem is the client learned nothing, whereas she *could* have learned so much about the state of her health simply by listening more. She could have left my office with a much deeper understanding of her situation and what to do about it. Instead she left knowing no more than when she came in.

Get the parallel? Does our incessant jabbering in prayer nauseate God? Would he like to perhaps get a word in edgewise? Does he just let us keep talking and talking? Yes. Do we fail to hear his voice that we might learn and mature? Yes.

Beware of extremes. Note that I am not saying, "Only listen," but "listen more," and there's a big difference. I am definitely not saying you should never speak to God, or that you should never ask him for things. Scripture is clear in commanding us to ask:

> *Ask, and it will be given to you; seek, and you will find; knock, and it will be opened to you. For everyone who asks receives, and the one who seeks finds, and to the one who knocks it will be opened.* (Matthew 7:7-8)

> *You do not have because you do not ask.* (James 4:2b)

If you're doing 90% of the talking in prayer, it's time to begin your radical prayer transformation by shutting your mouth.

RELATIONAL PRAYER

While we might begin embracing radical purpose in prayer with merely listening, obviously there's more to it than that. Prayer is the expression of a relationship with God. So then, what does it mean to have a relationship with someone, and what does it mean to practice "relational prayer?"

Relationships begin with spending time together. Think about whoever your best friend is. Imagine your only contact with that best friend being a one or two minute one-way conversation asking you for a number of things. At the conclusion of their laundry list of requests, they walk away terminating the meeting. How would you feel? Would you still view that as a valuable and meaningful relationship? Would you even still consider that person your friend?

News flash: God is a Person! In spite of that fact being central to our doctrinal orthodoxy, we often treat God like he's anything but a Person that has come to us in the most personable form with the incarnation of Christ. I know it's hard to relate to a person you cannot see or audibly hear, but God is a person who is present nevertheless. I am reminded of Isaiah 57:15:

> *For thus says the One who is high and lifted up, who inhabits eternity, whose name is Holy; I dwell in the high and holy place, and also with him who is of a contrite and lowly spirit, to revive the spirit of the lowly, and to revive the heart of the contrite.*

This passage contrasts the transcendence and the immanence of God. He is infinitely far above us (transcendent) and yet is also unbelievably close and present with us (immanent).

DIALOGUE NOT MONOLOGUE

Any good relationship is characterized by back and forth conversation. However, if one person does all the talking, you won't have much of a relationship. It is no different with God. Andrew Murray said:

> *Prayer is not monologue, but dialogue. God's voice in response to mine is its most essential part.*

Along the same line William McGill said:

> *The value of consistent prayer is not that He will hear us, but that we will hear Him.*

But just how does that "conversation" take place? After all, God isn't physically sitting next to you, and you don't audibly hear him as you would another person. The stock answer would be that God speaks to us through his word, the Bible, but let's expand on that a bit. There really are three "words" of God through which he may speak in our "conversation:"

1. Written Word of God – The Bible is more than just informational details about a variety of subjects. It is a supernatural book. It is the "breath of God" as noted in II Timothy 3:16. Countless Christians have testified throughout history of how the same Bible passage that had been repeatedly read over many years took on a new application at a particular time. It is an old book that continually becomes new through the energizing effect of the Spirit of God. Either by direct reference or by principle it speaks to all our deepest needs. If you want to hear God's side of the conversation in prayer, read the Bible, focusing on the passages most relevant to your concerns.

2. Creation Word of God – However, God doesn't only speak to us through the Bible, but also through his creation, according to Romans 1:18-20:

> *For the wrath of God is revealed from heaven against all ungodliness and unrighteousness of men, who by their*

> *unrighteousness suppress the truth. For what can be known about God is plain to them, because God has shown it to them. For his invisible attributes, namely, his eternal power and divine nature, have been clearly perceived, ever since the creation of the world, in the things that have been made. So they are without excuse.*

The creation screams of the presence and design of God. Have you ever just paused to contemplate the creation of God around you? Through it God is speaking, but are you listening? I remember walking on a rain dampened trail on a fall morning once when my eyes were drawn to the sun shining on a perfectly symmetrical spider web. It stopped me for several minutes as I considered the intricate design in that small part of God's creation. Did that spider web carry a message of God's presence? You bet!

Just being out in God's creation is almost guaranteed to increase your sense of the presence of God. In one of my previous book, *Face to Face: Meeting God in the Quiet Places*, I deal with the practice of Personal Retreats as a way to experience God and get his direction. Personal Retreats are largely based on the truth of God's presence in his creation, since most often they are done in more isolated places away from the man-made world. It's not that some message blasts into your head as you take a walk in woods so much as the quiet of nature allows you to experience God's presence without distraction.

3. Spirit Word of God – God speaks, not only through the Bible and the Creation, but through the indwelling Holy Spirit in believers. Jesus promised:

> *But the Helper, the Holy Spirt, whom the Father will send in my name, he will teach you all things and bring to your remembrance all that I have said to you.* (John 14:26)
>
> *When the Spirit of truth comes, he will guide you into all the truth, for he will not speak on his own authority, but whatever*

> *he hears he will speak, and he will declare to you the things that are to come.* (John 16:13)

These promises are precisely why it is so very important to **listen** in prayer. God is speaking through the Holy Spirit. However, one caveat: "Holy Spirit leading" has been credited with a multitude of falsehoods which God was in no way, shape or form involved in. We've all probably heard stories of professed Christians claiming the Holy Spirit led them to leave their spouses, commit adultery, defraud a business partner and the like. It is therefore mandatory that any "leading of the Holy Spirit" episodes in our lives be consistent with and backed up by the written Word of God. Anything else may be satanic deception or perhaps that inner urge was just plain indigestion!

DOES PRAYER CHANGE THINGS?

No discussion of prayer would be complete without pondering if or how prayer changes things. How do you imagine what happens when you petition God in prayer? Suppose you pray for safety on an upcoming trip. Do you imagine God, in effect, replying:

> *I am so glad you asked me to be with you and protect you on this trip. Because you looked to me, yes, I will protect you.*

What's wrong with this conception of God? First, it assumes that God has to be informed in order to focus his attention on our perceived needs. Second, it assumes that we know the best, most desirable course of action – namely, our being safe on the trip – even though we know many Christians are not kept safe in their travels. This view fails to ponder the greater purposes of God, as we will explore in the chapters that follow.

If we're honest, most of us would have to admit that we pray **in order to influence God**. What arrogance to assume that we have the power to change him who is (fortunately for us) unchangeable. Well, if prayer doesn't change what God is going to do, what is the point of it? Danish philosopher and theologian, Soren Kierkegaard nailed it when he said:

> ***The function of prayer is not to influence God, but rather to change the nature of the one who prays.***

I could almost end the whole book with that one simple statement. **The purpose of your spending time with God – communing with him – is not to change him, but to change you!** It is to conform and transform you into his image. Here's how the Apostle Paul put it:

> *For those whom he foreknew he also predestined to be conformed to the image of his Son, in order that he might be the firstborn among many brothers.* (Romans 8:29)

> *And we all, with unveiled face, beholding the glory of the Lord, are being transformed into the same image from one degree of glory to another. For this comes from the Lord who is the Spirit.* (II Corinthians 3:18)

This transformation requires adopting a radical purpose. But to understand God's purposes, we must understand his decrees. That's next.

APPLICATION & IMPLEMENTATION

1. For a few days spend the bulk of your time in prayer listening rather than speaking. Do you find you're experiencing more of God's presence?

2. How does your time talking to God in prayer compare with talking with a good friend?

THIS CHAPTER IN A NUTSHELL

1. We must first understand the purpose of prayer.

2. Listen more and talk less in prayer.

3. Prayer is primarily a means of building our relationship with God.

4. God speaks to us through his word, creation and Spirit.

5. "The purpose of prayer is not to influence God, but rather to change the nature of the one who prays." (Kierkegaard)

FOOTNOTES:

1. Crabb, Larry, *The PAPA Prayer*, p. xiii – xiv.

2. Keller, Timothy, *Prayer: Experiencing Awe and Intimacy with God*, (New York: Penguin Books), 2014, p. 77-78.

Chapter 2

Radical Decree

God has as much ordained His people's prayers as anything else, and when we pray we are producing links in the chain of ordained facts. – Charles Spurgeon

You will never experience a radical prayer transformation without first coming to a biblical understanding of God's decrees, which in turn are the key to praying according to his will, as we'll cover in the next chapter. Few subjects are more theologically daunting than the decrees of God. Mention God's decrees to the average Christian and prepare to be pelted with challenges like:

> So are we just robots then?

> What about my free will?

> God knows everything that will happen, but he doesn't decree it.

> How could God decree all the evil things in the world?

This topic is not only confusing, but, to the average untaught Christian, is downright offensive, being contrary to our natural way of thinking. Yet without some understanding of the decrees of God, not only will you be praying for the wrong things, but the question of why you should pray in the first place would be in serious doubt.

DEFINITION

Prayer according to God's will flows from God's decrees. Let's start with the definition of God's decrees from the Westminster Confession of Faith in 1646 – what is generally considered the most complete statement of Christian theology in the history of the church:

> *God, from all eternity, did, by the most wise and holy counsel of His own will freely, and unchangeably ordain whatsoever comes to pass: (1) yet so, as thereby neither is God the author of sin, nor is violence offered in the will of the creatures; nor is the liberty or contingency of second causes taken away, but rather established.*

What a mouthful! I realize that language may be challenging, so let's unpack this definition a bit and then show its basis in Scripture:

- God ordained before time began all that happens in time
- However, God decreed in such a way as he is not the creator of sin
- God decreed in such a way that no creature's will is forced by God to do something it doesn't desire to do (though I would hasten to add that God is very much in the business of changing hearts and resulting wills)
- Our actions are the "second causes" contemplated, given that the decree of God is always the first cause. To say that the decree of God "establishes" second causes, simply means that our actions are part of God's decree, that is, he decrees the means (our actions) as well as the end (resulting event).

The ultimate truth here is simply that God is sovereign, ruling over all things (Psalm 103:19). Theologically speaking, there really are but two views: the sovereignty of God or the sovereignty of man. Either God is in ultimate control or man is, relative to specific actions on earth. If the latter is the case, God not only is not sovereign, but is also not self-sufficient, since he would be essentially dependent, waiting to see what man will do in any given situation. In other words, God would cease to be God. Thankfully, that is not what we read in the Bible. Your view of God's decrees profoundly affects how you pray.

THE STORY GOD WROTE

While most Christians think of God as knowing the end of the story, the Bible goes further—**it teaches that God wrote the story**! Embracing the truth of God's decrees is not a matter of just subscribing to a man-made creed, but simply of reading what the Bible says:

> *I will tell of the decree: The LORD said to me, "You are my Son; today I have begotten you.* (Psalm 2:7)

I include the above verse primarily because it is the only passage in the Bible that uses the word "decree," though many passages deal with the concept. The decree that God the Father is speaking of concerns the incarnation of God the Son:

> *In him we have obtained an inheritance, having been predestined according to the purpose of him who works all things according to the counsel of his will.* (Ephesians 1:11)

This verse reminds us that God's purpose and will are paramount:

> *. . . for truly in this city there were gathered together against your holy servant Jesus, whom you anointed, both Herod and Pontius Pilate, along with the Gentiles and the peoples of Israel,* **to do whatever your hand and your plan had predestined to take place.** (Acts 4:27-28)

No passage could be clearer on the fact that God made a plan *previous* to the event spoken of and then executed it.

> *The lot is cast into the lap, but its every decision is from the LORD* (Prov. 16:33)

We like to think our decisions are strictly autonomous, perhaps like Jack in the movie, *Titanic*, yelling, "I'm the king of the world." By contrast this passage shows God's absolute and final control over all events. Unlike the deistic view of God as the Creator who has stepped back to only observe, the biblical view shows God involved in the smallest details of life.

> *Many are the plans in the mind of a man, but it is the purpose of the LORD that will stand.* (Proverbs 19:21)

Like the previous passage the supremacy of God's purpose and decree is what prevails:

> *The LORD of hosts has sworn: "As I have planned, so shall it be, and as I have purposed, so shall it stand . . . For the LORD of hosts has purposed, and who will annul it? His hand is stretched out, and who will turn it back?* (Isaiah 14:24, 27)

The purpose of God is spoken of again and again in these passages. No one can countermand his purposes.

> *I am God, and there is no other; I am God, and there is none like me, declaring the end from the beginning and from ancient times things not yet done, saying, "My counsel shall stand, and I will accomplish all my purpose," calling a bird of prey from the east, the man of my counsel from a far country. I have spoken, and I will bring it to pass; I have purposed, and I will do it.* (Isaiah 46:9b-11)

This ultimate control God has over events should delight, not dismay us. God tells us who he is and what he does. Such a God alone is worthy of our worship.

> *Our God is in the heavens; he does all that he pleases.* (Psalm 115:3)

Note the word "all" he pleases. We don't doubt that God does things, does amazing things and does supernatural things. The emphasis here is that he does 100% of what he intends, with his decrees never being defeated.

ELEMENTS OF GOD'S DECREES

Perhaps the best and most understandable teaching on the decrees of God comes from the late British theologian, A. W. Pink, in his classic work *The Nature of God*. In summary Pink identified the elements of God's decrees this way:[1]

- God's decrees concern all creatures and events
- Anything happening in time was foreordained before time began
- God's decree involves everything, whether small or great, good or evil
- Yet sin does not proceed from God by direct creation (as good does), but only by decretive permission and negative action. In other words part of God's decrees concerns the things he merely allows.

I remember a pastor preaching the Sunday after one of the school mass murders making the statement, "God didn't do that." Though I understood his sentiment, biblically speaking he was incorrect. Though the shooter's actions were not the result of God's positive decree, they were of a negative decree – they were an evil that God allowed to fulfill his greater (though unknown) purposes. Theologian R. C. Sproul notes:

*Because God is sovereign and His will can never be frustrated, we can be sure that nothing happens over which He is not in control. He at least must "permit" whatever happens to happen. He **chooses** to permit them in that He always has the power and right to intervene and prevent the actions and events of this world. Insofar as He lets things happen, He has "willed" them in this certain sense.*[2]

- God's decrees are his "hidden" will. We only learn God's decrees from observing the resulting events, just as we would learn an architect's plan by looking at the finished building. For example, we only know some person was "chosen before the foundation of the world" (Ephesians 1:4) to come to faith in Christ when that person actually does come to faith in Christ.

God's decrees are eternal, meaning they are outside of time. No decree of God is made "within time." Why? For God to decree something now – "within time" – would indicate that some new, uncontemplated event had happened requiring God to change his plans and decree something new. If such were the case, God would not be omniscient, but rather would be growing in knowledge with unfolding events. Likewise God would not be self-sufficient, since he would be dependent on the actions of man for determining his own actions. Obviously, if God were not omniscient and self-sufficient, he wouldn't be God at all, but merely a creation of our fallen minds. Yet incredibly, such a view has captured even formerly doctrinally orthodox theologians through the heresy of "open theism," which centers on a denial of God's omniscience.

GOD'S DECREES OR FOREKNOWLEDGE?

Does God actually decree things to happen, or does he just have foreknowledge of what actually will happen? Though the Bible rather clearly teaches the former, I think it's safe to say that most Christians today believe the latter, relegating God to the role of an observer of his creation. This is the view of deism rather than biblical Christianity. Jonathan Edwards attacked this subject in a different way, though, by showing that God's foreknowledge proves his decrees:

> *Whether God has decreed all things that ever come to pass or not, all that own the being of a God, own that He knows all things beforehand. Now it is self-evident that if He knows all things beforehand, He either doth approve of them or doth not approve of them; that is, He either is willing they should be, or He is not willing that they should be. But to will that they should be is to decree them.*[3]

Any way you cut it, God decrees. Without divine decrees you have no God.

SO WHY PRAY?

In terms of our radical prayer transformation the logical question arises:

> *If everything is already settled by God's decrees, why pray?*

Let's answer that by taking it even further – If everything is already settled, why do anything? Why eat, drink, breathe, move or work? The answer is really pretty simple. Those who deny a God who has decreed all things, ignore the meaning of "all" in "all things." God doesn't only decree the event, but also decrees prayer (and other human actions) in connection with those events. In other words **God decrees the means as well as the end.** For some events (probably a vast number of events in human history) God has decreed that prayer would indeed be the means by which those events occur. Charles Spurgeon nailed this truth in his classic sermon, "Prayer Certified of Success":

> *But another objection has been raised which is very ancient indeed, and has a great appearance of force. It is raised not so much by skeptics, as by those who hold a part of the truth; it is this – that prayer can certainly produce no results, because the decrees of God have settled everything, and those decrees are immutable. Now we have no desire to deny the assertion that the decrees of God have settled all events. It is our full belief that God has foreknown and predestinated everything that happeneth in heaven above or in the earth beneath, and that the foreknown station of a reed by the river is as fixed as the station of a king, and 'the chaff from the hand of the winnower is steered as the stars in their courses.' Predestination embraceth the great and the little, and reacheth unto all things; the question is, wherefore pray? Might it not as logically be asked wherefore breathe, eat, move, or do anything? We have an answer which satisfies us, namely, that our prayers are in the predestination, and that God has as much ordained His people's prayers as anything else, and when we pray we are producing links in the chain of ordained facts. Destiny decrees that I should pray—I pray; destiny decrees that I shall be answered, and the answer comes to me.*

Puritan Thomas Watson reflects the same sentiment:

> *The decree of God does not affect my endeavor; for he that decreed my salvation decreed it in the use of means, and if I neglect the means I reprobate myself. No man argues thus: God has decreed how long I shall live, therefore I will not use means to preserve my life, I will not eat and drink. God has decreed*

> *the time of my life in the use of means, so God has decreed my salvation in the use of the Word and of prayer. As a man who refuses food murders himself, so he that refuses to work out his salvation destroys himself. The vessels of mercy are said to be prepared unto glory (Rom 9:23). How are they prepared but by being sanctified? And that cannot be but in the use of means;* **therefore let not God's decree take thee off from holy endeavours.** *It is a good saying of Dr. Preston, "Hast thou a heart to pray to God? It is a sign no decree of wrath has passed against thee."*[4]

IF GOD DID NOT DECREE . . .

While many look at the decrees of God as constraining their freedom, it would actually be the lack of divine decree that would be tragic. Pink puts it this way:

> *To deny the divine decrees would be to predicate a world and all its concerns regulated by undesigned chance or blind fate. Then what peace, what assurance, what comfort would there be for our poor hearts and minds? What refuge would there be to fly to in the hour of trial? None at all. There would be nothing better than the black darkness and abject horror of atheism. How thankful we should be that everything is determined by infinite wisdom and goodness! What praise and gratitude are due unto God for His divine decrees. Because of them, "We know that all things work together for good to them that love God, to them who are the called according to his purpose" (Romans 8:28). Well may we exclaim, "For of him, and through him, and to him, are all things: to whom be glory forever. Amen"* (Romans 11:36).[4]

Knowing a God who has decreed all things catapults us to a different level of prayer and thus a radical prayer transformation. Instead of seeking to persuade God to fulfill our will, we now can seek the incredible privilege of participating in his will through prayer. But what is his will? We continue with radical will next.

APPLICATION & IMPLEMENTATION

1. When you approach God in prayer, consider the impact of his decrees on your life – your coming to faith, your daily sanctification and your ultimate eternal destiny.

2. Meditate on the Scriptures noted in this chapter which teach God's decrees. Do you gain any new insights on prayer after pondering these passages?

THIS CHAPTER IN A NUTSHELL

1. We must accept and understand that events flow from what God has purposed, not from what we want: What we usually pray to God is not that his will be done, but that he approves ours. (Helga Bergold Gross)

2. God's decrees determine and define his will.

3. Successful petitionary prayer will reflect his will, since God will not do anything contrary to his decreed will.

4. Thus to not know God's will when we pray guarantees failure.

FOOTNOTES:

1. A. W. Pink, *The Nature of God*, Chicago: Moody Press, 1975, 1999, p. 17-18.

2. R. C. Sproul, *Essential Truths of the Christian Faith*, Wheaton: Tyndale House, 1992, p. 67.

3. Pink, p. 20.

4. Thomas Watson, A *Body of Divinity*, Indo-European

Publishing, 2011, p. 595. Pink, p. 20

Chapter 3

Radical Will

The more we know God, the more we know God's will, the more likely our prayers will align with that will.[1] – Philip Yancey

In prayer, real prayer, we begin to think God's thoughts after him; to desire the things he desires, to love the things he loves, to will the things he wills.[2] – Richard Foster

After establishing that God has a decreed will, the next part of our radical prayer transformation is to line up with that will in our prayers. To pray other than within God's will is at best a waste of time and at worst rebellion against his authority. Praying according to God's will is perhaps best stated in I John 5:14-15:

> *And this is the confidence that we have toward him, that if we ask anything according to his will he hears us. And if we know that he hears us in whatever we ask, we know that we have the requests that we have asked of him.*

So, how might we interpret this passage? Let me give three possibilities:

> 1. Just pray whatever, knowing that when you luck out and happen to petition for something that is his will, it will be answered.

> 2. Again just pray whatever, but at the end of your petition tack on, "If it be your will" right before the Amen.

> 3. First determine what God's will is and then pray for its fulfillment.

Like most Christians, I spent most of the earlier part of my Christian life doing either #1 or #2, and consequently really didn't find much in the way of either results or joy from my prayer life.

Why do we pray that way? Part of it involves our misunderstanding of just what prayer is and is not. If we have a conception of God as one with no set plan who is sitting in heaven, waiting to be persuaded by us to do something, we'll ask for all manner of things without considering their divine legitimacy. I am convinced that **most Christians are wishing instead of praying**. A love song popular in the 1950's called "Maybe," written by Richard Barrett and performed by The Chantels captures this sentiment:

> *Maybe, if I pray every night*
> *You'll come back to me*
> *And maybe, if I cry everyday*
> *You'll come back to stay*
> *Oh, maybe . . .*
> *I've prayed and prayed to the Lord*
> *To send you back, my love*
> *But instead you came to me*
> *Only in my dreams*

But it's not just "wishing" instead of praying. Sometimes we tend to be arrogant with God, in effect assuming that he needs our cajoling to come to the right decisions! It would be a bit like being chosen to be in play someone else wrote, but continually demanding re-writes of the script. Like it or not, scripture makes clear that the script is already written. We just need to learn our part and play our part through the insight and strength the Holy Spirit provides.

We also pray in these ineffective ways out of sheer laziness. It's easy to just throw out whatever is on your mind by way of requests when praying, giving little or no thought to whether said petitions are biblically legitimate. Biblical prayer, as I am teaching in this book, is not easy. It is work and is probably some of the hardest work you'll ever do, though I would hasten to add that it is a work you will fall in love with.

CONFIDENCE IN PRAYER

Let's break down I John 5:14-15. It begins with **confidence** in prayer. How confident are you when you pray? Are you 100% convinced God is going to grant your petition? 80%? 50%? Not confident at all? Do you really expect prayer to "work," or do you just do it out of habit or a sense of biblical duty?

John says our confidence in prayer comes from praying according to God's will. If you know that the sovereign, omnipotent God wills to do something, and know that his decreed will according to the Scriptures cited in the previous chapter always prevails, what can that do for you but give you absolute confidence in what you're praying for? The whole dynamic is changed from the unknown (I wish God would do this) to the known (I know God will do this).

Here's another way of thinking about this: Suppose you are the Press Secretary to the President of the United States. Does it make a difference when you go out to the Briefing Room if you absolutely know the mind of the President on an issue you are addressing? If his "will" is crystal clear, you have no problem stating his position to the press. But if his position is fuzzy or he hasn't told you, you won't have that same confidence. Prayer is no different. It is a delight to pray, absolutely knowing the decreed will of God, but exceedingly frustrating if you don't.

HEARING PRAYER

So what does this mean? Since God is omniscient, he obviously "hears" everything. It's not like we're talking on a frequency God isn't tuned into. The sense of "hearing" prayer refers to God responding positively to a petition. When the Psalmist says, "Hear my cry, O LORD (Psalm

61:1) or "Give ear to my prayer, O God" (Psalm 55:1), he isn't suggesting that he needs to wake God up from sleep or get his attention. The sense of God "hearing" is captured by David in Psalm 4:1:

> *Answer me when I call, O God of my righteousness! You have given me relief when I was in distress. Be gracious to me and hear my prayer!*

The idea is simply that he is seeking an affirmative answer to his petition.

KNOW WE HAVE THE REQUESTS

When is the last time after praying for something you **knew** your request was granted? Some would probably say they never have had that assurance, though they **hoped** their request would be granted. The passage is not speaking of wishing or hoping something would happen, but **knowing** it would happen. It speaks of an absolute certainty. Isn't that the experience you want in prayer?

A RADICAL IDEA?

May I present a radical "what if" to you for your prayer transformation? What if you just prayed for things you know to be God's will? How would that change your prayer life? What would be the difference between praying with uncertainty and just hoping your prayer is affirmatively answered versus praying something you know to be God's will, for which you have complete assurance of an answer? Imagine the difference in your confidence! Would that catapult you into a "whatever you pray believing you will receive" (Matthew 21:22) experience? Would you perhaps identify with the experience of Martin Luther, who said:

> *Lord, I will have my will of thee at this time. I will have my will, for I know that my will is thy will.*

KNOWING GOD'S WILL

We now come to the question of how do we know what God's will is? If we commit to focusing our prayer life on the known will of God, just how do we know what that is? Let me propose four ways:

1. Passages That Directly Say, "This is God's will" – This is fairly easy since there are only three verses in the New Testament that directly say what God's will is. Here they are:

> *For this is the will of God, your sanctification: that you abstain from sexual immorality; that each one of you know how to control his own body in holiness and honor, not in the passion of lust like the Gentiles who do not know God; that no one transgress and wrong his brother in this matter, because the Lord is an avenger in all these things, as we told you beforehand and solemnly warned you. For God has not called us for impurity, but in holiness.* (I Thessalonians 4:3-7)

We absolutely know from this passage that God's will is our sanctification, that is, our being set apart for holiness. The specific context of the passage relates to sexual immorality, but it certainly could be applied to all areas of personal holiness. To petition God relative to your own sanctification or to that of another believer is clearly his will which can be prayed with full confidence of an answer.

Our second definite "will of God" passage comes from the same epistle:

> *Rejoice always, pray without ceasing, give thanks in all circumstances; for this is the will of God in Christ Jesus for you.* (I Thessalonians 5:16-18)

Though I used to just focus on the single "will of God" admonition in verse 18, I now see that there are really three things stated as God's will for us – rejoicing, praying and giving thanks. Though there are three, I think they are tied together relative to specific trials experienced. When things are difficult it is God's will that we rejoice, that we continually pray and that we give thanks. We rejoice because, no matter how challenging our circumstances might be, we are recipients of the grace of God – chosen, called, regenerated, forgiven, empowered and sanctified – no matter what trial we are facing.

We pray without ceasing in those situations because prayer is our connection and communion with God who is the source for all our needs. We give thanks because God is sovereign over whatever we're going through and promises to work all circumstances, even the most evil ones, for our good (Romans 8:28). There's really quite a lot to pray about in that one passage and to be totally confident of God affirmatively responding.

The third "will of God" passage is found in I Peter 2:13-17:

> *Be subject for the Lord's sake to every human institution, whether it be to the emperor as supreme, or to governors as sent by him to punish those who do evil and to praise those who do good. For this is the will of God, that by doing good you should put to silence the ignorance of foolish people. Live as people who are free, not using your freedom as a cover-up for evil, but living as servants of God. Honor everyone. Love the brotherhood. Fear God. Honor the emperor.*

This passage speaks primarily of Christians being in submission to political authority, as opposed to being viewed as insurrectionists, echoing Paul's message in Romans 13. It is not merely an instruction, but an admonition with the promise that our submission would be a testimony to unbelievers, silencing them from viewing us as political radicals. Prayers for civil authorities and our appropriate submission to said authorities are the known will of God for which we can pray confidently.

2. General Statements Defining God's Will – Many, many

passages in scripture teach us what God's will is without specifically saying, "This is God's will," as the three passages above do. Obviously there is a lot more scripture in this category. Let's start with Ephesians 4:1-3:

> *I therefore, the prisoner for the Lord, urge you to walk in a manner worthy of the calling to which you have been called, with all humility and gentleness, with patience, bearing with one another in love, eager to maintain the unity of the Spirit in the bond of peace.*

Any Christian can pray the following from this passage for themselves (or another believer) with full assurance of praying in God's will:

- Walk in humility, gentleness and patience
- Show forbearance in love with those we have difficulty with
- Maintain unity of the Spirit in the Body of Christ

Most of us are deficient, to one degree or another in these attributes, and yet, since these are things God definitely wills, we are guaranteed he will hear and answer prayer for these behaviors.

How about Colossians Chapter 3, which begins:

> *If then you have been raised with Christ, seek the things that are above, where Christ is, seated at the right hand of God. Set your minds on things that are above, not on things that are on earth.*

A long list of "God-willed prayers" can be compiled from this chapter, including praying for:

- A mind focused on heavenly things
- Putting to death sexual immorality, impurity, passion, evil desire and covetousness.
- Putting away of anger, wrath, malice, slander, obscene talk and lying

- Putting on compassion, kindness, humility, meekness, patience and love
- Bearing with and forgiving one another
- Experiencing Christ's peace in your heart
- Allowing Christ's word to indwell richly
- Being thankful
- And more

All of these things can be prayed for with full confidence, and yet we don't tend to pray this way, that is, we don't pray the way Paul prayed. Why? **I think we would rather pray for our own personal desires – the stuff we want right now – than pray for what God wants for us.** It really gets down to whether we see God as someone to help fulfill our plans or see ourselves as instruments to fulfill his plans.

3. Prayers in Scripture – Perhaps the richest source of knowing how to pray the will of God is simply praying the prayers in scripture, knowing it is the inspired Word of God. A good place to start is the Psalms, most of which are prayers. The prayers of Hannah, Daniel and others are also exemplary, as we'll cover in a later chapter. In addition to Paul's prayers in the epistles cited above, Jesus' high priestly prayer in John 17 gives additional insights. In these, of course, we have to discern what aspects of the prayer were specific to that person in that situation versus the universally applicable features of their prayers.

4. Impressions of the Holy Spirit – This is admittedly dangerous ground, being an area subject to much deception. Untold numbers of books could be written about people who said, "God told me . . ." and didn't know the leading of the Holy Spirit from indigestion! Yet we cannot close the door and deny that God the Holy Spirit isn't still speaking, "guiding us into all truth" (John 16:13). Though most of his speaking to us is through the written word, he can and does impress people directly. This requires a deep, mature connection with God and the ability to confirm the "leading" through scripture.

Knowing God willed to do something, purely by the impression of the Holy Spirit, is a most blessed, though usually rare experience. I have experienced this but a few times. The one that stands out the most in my mind was in 1976 when I had just started writing my first book, *Eat, Drink & Be Ready*. I was with a major Christian ministry at the time that frankly wasn't really keen on its staff writing books. It specifically had a policy against granting leaves of absence for that purpose. Yet I was convinced that I had to get away for a couple of months to focus specifically on writing. In praying about that situation I clearly felt led that it was God's will that I have the leave of absence. I wrote up the request and submitted it to the personnel department with full confidence it would be granted. It was. It was an amazing experience, but only rarely the way God has worked in my life.

FAITH & PRAYER

Praying according to God's will has another amazing benefit – it generates faith. Jesus taught that believing prayer is answered:

> *And whatever you ask in prayer, you will receive, if you have faith.* (Matthew 21:22)

> *Therefore I tell you, whatever you ask in prayer, believe that you have received it, and it will be yours.* (Mark 11:24)

Think of it this way: Prayer Request A is for something you wish would happen, but you don't really know if it's God's will. Prayer Request B is for something you know from scripture is definitely God's will. With which prayer will you have more faith? Obviously, Prayer Request B. When you start focusing your prayer petitions on things you don't merely wish for, but rather know are God's will, you will discover what praying believing really means. It adds a whole new dimension to your prayer experience.

CONCLUSION

I can give no greater exhortation than encouraging prayer according to God's will. Such prayer puts us in the necessary right position before our Creator – as subjects of the Sovereign One who has written the story in which we are characters. When we allow his will to become our will, we will see amazing things happen in prayer. A classic collection of Puritan prayers puts it this way:

> *Let me know that the work of prayer is to bring my will to thine, and that without this it is folly to pray; when I try to bring thy will to mine it is to command Christ, to be above him, and wiser than he: this is my sin and pride.*[1]

APPLICATION & IMPLEMENTATION

1. For the next week limit your prayer petitions to those which you know to be the will of God. Observe what happens to your faith.

2. Read through Ephesians and Colossians, noting from Paul's prayers the things that are God's will. Then pray these for yourself and other believers.

THIS CHAPTER IN A NUTSHELL

1. Only prayer that is according to God's decreed will is answered.

2. Prayer not according to God's will is wishing, not praying.

3. God's will may be determined through specific scriptures, general scriptures, creation and biblically sound impressions from the Holy Spirit.

4. Prayer according to God's will generates confidence and faith in an answer.

FOOTNOTES:

1. Arthur Bennett, Editor, *The Valley of Vision: A Collection of Puritan Prayer & Devotions*, (Carlisle, PA: The Banner of Truth Trust, 1975, p. 266.

Chapter 4

Radical Praise

In prayer we act like men; in praise we act like angels – Thomas Watson

I remember meeting one guy years ago who punctuated his sentences with saying, "Praise the Lord!" as apparently his way of expressing his spirituality. I hope you don't think me too unspiritual, but after a couple minutes of that I was ready to throw up. Is saying, "Praise the Lord!" actually what is meant by praising God? I think (and I hope) it's something far more.

Over 200 verses in the Bible speak of praising God, the bulk of them being in the Psalms. We are exhorted repeatedly to "praise the Lord," but what does that really mean? More importantly, is praising God a major part of your prayer life? If it isn't, you're missing what is probably the most important part of prayer.

WHAT PRAISE IS NOT

One of the best ways to understand the meaning of praising God is to explain what it is NOT. Praise is NOT thanksgiving. Make no mistake, thanksgiving is an important part of prayer, but it is distinct from praise. Ever been at a prayer meeting where the leader says, "Let's begin by praising God." I guarantee that what will almost always follow is not *praising* God, but *thanking* God. Frankly, thanking God (or anyone else) is a whole lot easier than praising that person. That's why we don't more easily practice praise. We thank God for *doing* something for us. Praise is a very different thing.

Imagine two different situations between a husband and wife: In the first, one spouse *thanks* the other for taking out the garbage or doing the dishes. Now that's nice and maybe makes them feel slightly appreciated, but that's about it. It's neither memorable nor exciting, and it certainly doesn't advance any great intimacy in the relationship. That's thanksgiving.

But let's take another encounter between husband and wife in which one says to the other, "You are amazing! I am overwhelmed by your love and care for me." I guarantee your response will be a bit different than being thanked for taking out the garbage or doing the dishes. You won't forget this and the intimacy of the relationship will increase. That's praise.

As referred to earlier, praise is also NOT just saying, "Praise the Lord!" That phrase is an imperative, that is, a command to do something. Saying, "Praise the Lord," therefore is NOT actually praising God, but simply telling someone else that they should praise him. Following through with our marriage illustration, it would be like saying, "Love your wife!" Imagine at your house going around all day saying to your wife, "Love your wife!" "Love your wife!" Again, that's simply a command for someone to love their wife. I know it's hard to believe, but that won't actually deepen your marriage. Saying, "Love your wife" isn't actually loving your wife. The idea is to actually *do* the action of loving.

WHAT PRAISE IS

Let's start with a dictionary definition of praise[1]:

1. To set a price on; appraise
2. To commend the worth of; express approval or admiration of
3. To laud the glory of (God, etc.) as in song; glorify; extol

I am often amazed at how an English dictionary can be an outstanding Bible study tool. I never before noticed that the familiar word "appraise" was a form of the word "praise." To praise God is to set a price on what he is worth, by describing his attributes and their worth. For our purposes I would define the praise of God this way:

> ***Praise is a worshipful confession to God of who he is and what he does.***

Praise is saying to God, "You are . . ." It focuses on his attributes – his holiness, power, knowledge, sovereignty, love, mercy, etc. The same idea, though not to the same degree, would be true of praise on a human level, as with a spouse. Though you can't praise your spouse's omnipotence, omniscience or sovereignty, you can praise their love, mercy or kindness.

While praise begins with "You are . . ." thanksgiving says to God, "You did . . ." Praise is focused on *attributes*, while thanksgiving focuses on *actions*.

PURPOSE OF PRAISE

I don't want to stop with the mere exhortation to praise God. It helps greatly to know **why** praising God is so emphasized (and commanded) in Scripture. I think it is as simple as this:

Praise builds your relationship with God

Essentially praise takes your relationship with God (or really anyone else) to the next level. Sometimes we forget that God is a Person, not merely some force. Persons have relationships with one another. So the question is, "What is the 'level' of your relationship with God?" Is it shallow or deep? Superficial or profound? Distant or intimately close? I think we can get a handle on the level of relationships with a continuum called the **Seven A's.**

THE SEVEN A'S

Your relational depth, not only with God, but with every single person on earth can be defined and measured by the Seven A's, as you simply ask where you are on its continuum:

1. Acknowledgement – This is the first step in a relationship – simply acknowledging the existence of another person. With most of the several billion people on the planet, you haven't gotten to acknowledgment yet, in that you don't know who they are, having never met them. When you are first introduced to someone, you are at the acknowledgment level of the relationship. Acknowledgment isn't really worth much by itself, but it is where all relationships start. You may move past acknowledgment in 30 seconds or remain stuck on it for 30 years, depending on whether you move up the relationship continuum.

An example of acknowledgment would be the typical "greeting" time at the beginning of a church service where you shake hands and say, "Good morning," but that's where it ends. I'm essentially saying that I acknowledge you are a person occupying space in my vicinity. However, a few more words can take the relationship up to the next level.

2. Acceptance – Acceptance takes the relationship a bit farther. At this stage you're essentially saying, "You're okay to be in my presence and for me to talk to." Some positive input, albeit small, has been expressed to get you out of mere acknowledgment. This might be thought of as the "acquaintance" level of relationship. I know who you are, I don't have any particular problem with you, but I wouldn't really consider you a friend. Acceptance is really fairly bland and nothing to get that excited about. The next two levels on the Seven A's will, however, actually move you into a friendship.

Back to our example at church, acceptance happens when after that acknowledgement greeting, you communicate some positive emotion about that person being there. Acceptance is to regard favorably. That might be done through words or even a smile. The guy that usually sits in front of me in church does neither, so we're still at acknowledgment I'm afraid!

3. Approval – The central idea of approval in relationships is communicating that something is worthy or good. To approve of someone is to say, "Amen" to them and what they have done. It reflects a basic agreement with that person. For example if I send a link to an article I've written to my pastor and he responds by expressing agreement with what I've written, that is approval. While acceptance is largely a neutral expression of "You're okay to be in my presence," approval is a more specific agreement to my actions.

4. Appreciation – With appreciation we move even deeper. To appreciate you or something you've done means not merely that I approve of it, but that I am helped by it. In appreciation I am acknowledging that you have actually *done* something to my benefit.

5. Admiration – In this fifth step in our continuum, I am holding you in high esteem. It's not just that I approve or appreciate, but that I really think you are someone special. With this fifth "A" we are moving beyond looking at the "what you do" more to the "who you are."

6. Affection – The dictionary defines affection as a warm and tender feeling toward someone. To have affection is to deeply like someone. This is very personal and largely not connected to favorable or unfavorable actions.

7. Adoration – With adoration we have an even greater level of intimate relationship. The dictionary would describe this as "loving greatly" or "honoring highly." When applied to someone other than God, adoration may border on idolatry. To say the least, it can only appropriately characterize a very few close relationships.

So what do the Seven A's have to do with praising God? **The idea of praise is to get you to the seventh A – adoration.** As I said earlier, you can determine your level of relationship with every person in the world on the Seven A's continuum. But you can also apply it to your relationship with God:

    Acknowledgement – You believe God exists

    Acceptance – You are tolerant of his existence

    Approval – You recognize his providential working in the world

    Appreciation – You are pleased with his blessings in your life

    Admiration – You are related to him in a love relationship

    Affection – You have developed a deep love toward God

    Adoration – You praise and worship him for who he is

In this continuum you probably are not a believer until you get at least to step 5 – admiration. You're a mature believer at step 7 –

adoration and praise. Apart from a relationship of praise you cannot deeply know God.

LEARNING PRAISE FROM DAVID

Without a doubt the Psalms present the greatest number of examples of praising God. Of course, most of the Psalms were written by David, the man after God's own heart. Isn't it interesting that the man we especially associate with intimately knowing God was the man who wrote the most scripture praising God? Knowing God intimately and praising him intensely are inseparable. Do you really want to learn how to praise God? Just study the Psalms.

One of my favorite examples is Psalm 145, where we read in the first seven verses:

> *I will extol you, my God and King, and bless your name forever and ever. Every day I will bless you and praise your name forever and ever. Great is the LORD, and greatly to be praised, and his greatness is unsearchable. One generation shall commend your works to another, and shall declare your mighty acts. On the glorious splendor of your majesty, and on your wondrous works, I will meditate. They shall speak of the might of your awesome deeds, and I will declare your greatness. They shall pour forth the fame of your abundant goodness and shall sing aloud of your righteousness.*

Guess what? These first seven verses are really **not** an example of praising God. Note that David keeps saying, "I will" and "They shall." He speaks of something that hasn't happened yet – He is simply saying that he is *going* to praise God. The actual praise is what follows:

> *The LORD is gracious and merciful, slow to anger and abounding in steadfast love. The LORD is good to all, and his mercy is over all that he has made . . . Your kingdom is an everlasting kingdom, and your dominion endures throughout all generations. The LORD is faithful in all his words and kind in all his works. The LORD upholds all who are falling and raises up all who are bowed down. The eyes of all look to you, and you give them their food in due season. You open your hand*

and satisfy the desire of every living thing. The LORD is righteous in all his ways and kind in all his works. The LORD is near to all who call upon him in truth. He fulfills the desire of those who fear him; he also hears their cry and saves them. The LORD preserves all who love him, but all the wicked he will destroy. (Psalm 145:8-9, 13-20)

Note the repetition of "The LORD is . . ." This is the key to recognizing praise versus thanksgiving. He focuses on who God is and simply cites the "what he does" as examples of God's character and attributes.

If we have any doubt that this is a passage of praise to God, David actually tells us so in verse 21:

My mouth will speak the praise of the LORD, and let all flesh bless his holy name forever and ever.

So much can be mined out of this one Psalm to learn how to praise God. Scores of other Psalms will teach you even further. Remember that when you read the Psalms you are "eavesdropping" on David's intimate communication with God. They represent the highest form of prayer. Imitate them and experience a praise transformation. Praise sets you up for perhaps the highest form of prayer. We tackle that next.

APPLICATION & IMPLEMENTATION

1. For the next week, focus your prayer life on praying the Psalms and observe how your intimacy with God changes.

2. Ponder which attributes of God are impacting you the most right now and then begin praising him by saying, "You are . . ."

THIS CHAPTER IN A NUTSHELL

1. Praise is not thanksgiving, nor saying "Praise the Lord!"

2. Praise is a worshipful confession to God of who he is and what he does.

3. Praise builds intimacy in your relationship with God.

4. The Psalms represent our greatest instruction in how to praise God.

Chapter 5

Radical Meditation

Prayer is when you talk to God; meditation is when you listen to God
— Author Unknown

Whatever happened to meditation? What radical transformative change can meditation produce in our prayer life? While there are numerous biblical references to the practice, it is not central to the life of most Christians, as J. I. Packer said:

> *... meditation is a lost art today, and Christian people suffer grievously from their ignorance of the practice.*

I think meditation was "hijacked." The word "meditation" to the average person conjures up images of eastern religions whose theologies Christians appropriately reject. I think meditation has thus become "guilty by association."

The biblical concept of meditation is totally different than that of eastern religions. It is not sitting in some contorted position chanting, "Ommmmmmmmmmmmmmmmmm." Biblical meditation focuses on God, his Word and his promises, while eastern meditation focuses on nothingness – on emptying the mind. Buddhism's goal is basically to become nothing. Frankly, I take that by faith – we are nothing, at least apart from the Christ-life put into us at our spiritual regeneration.

I don't know of a practice that promises more benefits than biblical meditation. We read in Joshua 1:8:

> *This Book of the Law shall not depart from your mouth, but you shall meditate on it day and night, so that you may be careful to do according to all that is written in it. For then you will make your way prosperous, and then you will have good success.*

How about Psalm 119:99:

> *I have more understanding than all my teachers, for your testimonies are my meditation.*

Wow! It says that meditation leads to obedience, and that obedience results in prosperity and success. Who doesn't want that? How about having more understanding than your teachers? Meditation lines us up with God's thoughts and ways. As that alignment occurs, life simply works better.

Meditation is basically a form of prayer, perhaps the highest form of prayer. Is it any wonder that we have anemic prayer lives when we're missing that superior type of prayer? Granted, we need to practice meditation, but first we have to know what it is.

WHAT IS MEDITATION?

J. I. Packer defines meditation this way:

> *Meditation is the activity of calling to mind, and thinking over, and dwelling on, and applying to oneself, the various things that one knows about the works and ways and purposes and promises of God. It is an activity of holy thought, consciously performed in the presence of God, under the eye of God, by the help of God, as a means of communion with God.*

Tim Keller notes:

> *. . . meditation is taking the truth down into our hearts until it catches fire there and begins to melt and shape our reactions to God, ourselves, and the world.*[1]

I like to think of meditation as "applied praise." Like praise, meditation focuses on who God is and what he has done. It is an unhurried contemplation and reflection upon the truth of God and his word. Charles Spurgeon adds some additional ideas to the concept:

> *There are times when solitude is better than company and silence is wiser than speech. We would be better Christians if we were alone more often, waiting on God and gathering, through meditation of His Word, spiritual strength for His service. We are spiritually fed when we think on the things of God. Truth is like a cluster of grapes. If we want wine we must bruise, press, and squeeze it many times. The bruiser's feet must come down joyfully on the grapes, or else the juice will not flow. They must tread the grapes well, or else much of the precious liquid will be wasted. So must we by meditation tread the clusters of truth if we would get the wine of consolation.*

The dictionary defines "meditation" this way:

1. To reflect upon; study; ponder
2. Solemn reflection on sacred matters as a devotional act

Two Hebrew words are translated "meditation" in the Old Testament:

   1. *hagah* – to moan, growl, utter, speak

This word is used seven times in the Old Testament, including Joshua 1:8 (quoted above) and Psalm 63:6.

   2. *siach* – to muse, complain, talk of

This Hebrew word is used eleven times in the Old Testament, including Psalm 77:6 and Psalm 119: 15, 23, 27, 48, 78, 97, 99, 148.

OF SHEEP AND RUMINATION

The key to understanding meditation is to understand sheep and their digestion. Meditation parallels the rumination process in cud-chewing animals. The English Reformation leader, Thomas Cranmer, upon losing his wife and baby in childbirth said:

> *Let us ruminate [on Scripture], as it were, chew the cud, so we may have its sweet juice, spiritual effect, marrow, honey, kernel, taste, comfort and consolation.*

A 12th century abbot in France, Hugh St. Victor, noted that scriptural food:

is solid stuff, and, unless it be well chewed, it cannot be swallowed

Rumination is a complicated digestive process compared to that of humans, which involves four "stomachs" and over 40,000 chewing jaw movements per day. Each of these four stomachs has a definite application to meditation:

1. Reticulum – The first "stomach" is basically a fermentation vat, featuring a honeycombed structure to help bring food boluses back up for further chewing, as well as catching foreign objects for expulsion.

2. Rumen – Using strong contractions the rumen acts as a mixing chamber that adds beneficial microorganisms. These probiotics synthesize protein and B vitamins. Like the reticulum, the rumen also removes waste products.

3. Omasum – The first two "stomachs" are preparatory in nature. In the omasum nutrient absorption actually begins. It is structured like pages in a book with the many surfaces absorbing fatty acids and electrolytes.

4. Abomasum – This is the true stomach. Like the omasum, it has more page-like leaves for nutrient absorption. It also secretes hydrochloric acid and enzymes to break down proteins, just as in the human digestive system.

Summarizing the sheep (or other ruminant's) digestive process, we first observe it is most extensive. Actually it takes 24 hours for food to become flesh in a ruminant, as compared to a non-cud chewing animal like a pig where only two hours is required. Incidentally I would add that is part of the "health basis" behind the Old Testament Dietary Law, namely, keeping people away from the more toxic meats (which was documented in 1953 by David Macht, MD at Johns Hopkins Medical School and published in the *Bulletin of the History of Medicine*).

In this digestive process we see lots and lots of chewing in order to properly break the food down. Along with that we observe the removal of foreign objects that were accidentally picked up in grazing. Finally we see greater absorption of nutrients as a result of this prolonged process.

APPLICATION TO MEDITATION

We've studied the digestive process of a sheep, but how does that apply to the radical meditation commanded in the Bible? Here are six parallels:

- God's Person and Word require extensive digestion to get the full benefit
- We must take time for the Word to "ferment" before its truths (nutrients) come out.
- To really get the full message we must chew and chew and chew on it.
- Instead of our "chewing" purifying the Word, it purifies us as we chew on it.
- Only after the extensive process of meditation are we fully nourished
- Without meditation we will be deficient in spiritual nutrients

THE SUMMER I LEARNED MEDITATION

I learned more about meditation from watching cows and goats chew their cud than from any other source. My wife and I spent the summer of 1976 in her grandparents second home along the Wilson River in the dairy country of Tillamook, Oregon. From our kitchen table I would look out on the cows grazing and then chewing their cud in the adjacent pasture. The more I watched them, the more fascinated I became with the sheer amount of time they spent at cud chewing.

But another thing impressed me: they were so relaxed and unhurried. It relaxed me to watch them. By instinct those cows knew this behavior was essential to survival. Would that we learned the similar necessity of meditating on God and his Word! To not meditate, to not chew our spiritual cud – our partially digested spiritual food –

leads to spiritual indigestion and spiritual nutrient deficiencies.

BUT HOW DO YOU DO IT?

First recognize that meditation takes time, which is probably the main reason we don't do it. Most people, though probably fewer and fewer, know that consuming a meal takes time, unless you want a lot of indigestion. To meditate on a verse or passage of scripture requires simply "chewing" it over and over again. Think about it as you say it over and over again in your mind or verbally.

Memorizing it is one of the best ways to prepare you for meditating on the passage. As a senior in college when I was a relatively new Christian, I attended a most amazing weekend retreat. The speaker, rather than give the usual messages, instead had us memorize the first chapter of the Epistle of James. I can't even begin to describe the insights that came from that memorization and the subsequent meditation it facilitated. The truths of James 1 bonded to my soul in a way that has taken me through nearly 50 years of trials and temptations – all from just one chapter of one book. That is a radical concept. It is powerful!

We tend to read the Bible in a fairly superficial way most of the time. When you find a verse that really speaks to your current need, just stop and meditate upon it. Two basic questions to ask as you ponder the passage:

> **1. What does the passage mean?** How would its original readers have understood it? Study the meaning of its key words and look up cross references to better understand what is being said.

> **2. How would God apply this passage to me?** Once you understand what the passage is saying, you then have to figure out how it applies to you. How does this passage convict you, encourage you, inspire you or comfort you?

Chew it over and over again until its full implications are impacting you. Devote an unhurried time to that small portion of Scripture and try to extract every last bit of spiritual nutrition from it. That's how you meditate. You will be amazed at the insights that come from that process. Meditation is not the end of the prayer process, however. It will lead to our next radical prayer concept.

APPLICATION & IMPLEMENTATION

1. Each day for the next week, take a few minutes to meditate on a Bible verse you find particularly relevant to your current needs. Observe the additional insights that meditation produces.

2. Next memorize a small passage and note how that affects your ability to meditate upon the passage.

THIS CHAPTER IN A NUTSHELL

1. Biblical meditation is not practiced by most Christians today.

2. Meditation is the unhurried contemplation and reflection upon the truth of God and his Word.

3. Meditation is the same idea as "cud chewing" in ruminant animals.

4. Meditation allows you to more fully extract the full spiritual nutrition from God's Word.

FOOTNOTES:

1. Keller, Timothy, *Prayer: Experiencing Awe and Intimacy with God*, (New York: Penguin Books, 2014), p. 151.

Chapter 6

Radical Confession

We must move from asking God to take care of the things that are breaking our hearts, to praying about the things that are breaking His heart. – Margaret Gibb

What if you were to come face to face with God right now? What do you think your reaction would be? In the Bible we see examples of that very thing, such as the experience of Isaiah:

> *In the year that King Uzziah died I saw the Lord sitting upon a throne, high and lifted up; and the train of his robe filled the temple. Above him stood the seraphim. Each had six wings: with two he covered his face, and with two he covered his feet, and with two he flew. And one called to another and said: "Holy, holy, holy is the LORD of hosts; the whole earth is full of his glory!" And the foundations of the thresholds shook at the voice of him who called, and the house was filled with smoke. And I said: "Woe is me! For I am lost; for I am a man of unclean lips, and I dwell in the midst of a people of unclean lips; for my eyes have seen the King, the LORD of hosts!"* (Isaiah 6:1-5)

Is it not fascinating that the first reaction to a "God encounter" is confession of sin? Prayers of confession stand as one of the most familiar forms of prayer practiced by Christians, not to mention being part of the order of worship in liturgical churches. Ideally prayers of confession should flow from meditation, wherein we expand our concept of the majesty of God. In meditation we grasp God's great worthiness which dramatically increases awareness of our own unworthiness. What could be a more logical response to seeing God than confession of sin?

But do we really understand confession? Exactly what purpose does confessing our sins serve? What is the role of confession in prayer? Most importantly, what is the biblical way of confession?

CONFESSION DEFINED

The most familiar passage concerning confession of sin is I John 1:9:

> *If we confess our sins, he is faithful and just to forgive us our sins and to cleanse us from all unrighteousness.*

The Greek word translated "confess" is *homologeo*, which is actually a combination of two words: *homo*, meaning "same" and *logos*, meaning "word." Thus, to confess is to say the "same word" as God – to agree with God concerning our sin. While a child may confess a misdeed to an unknowing parent, God always knows everything about our sin in advance and has judged it as such. Confession therefore, is not *informing* God of anything he doesn't already know, but simply saying the "same word" back to him.

CONFESSION PURPOSE

So why do we confess sin if God already knows about it, and Christ has already paid for it with his sacrificial death? Confession certainly is not to "get" forgiveness – we already have that if we have trusted in Christ. The purpose of confession of sin is to "experience" forgiveness. When we sin it is not our *relationship* with God that is broken, but rather our *fellowship* with him. Like the Prodigal Son, who was always the son of his father, we return to God and confess our sin to renew our fellowship.

Note that the Apostle John says confession *cleanses* us from unrighteousness. This hearkens to the Old Testament ceremonial law, wherein cleansing was required *before* coming into the presence of God in worship. We see this is the pattern of the Tabernacle and later, the Temple. After sacrificing at the brazen altar (now fulfilled in Christ), one would next come to the laver for ceremonial washing. Only after washing did the priest enter the tabernacle or temple itself. Likewise we approach God after being cleansed by the confession of our sin.

CONFESSION MOTIVATION

Not all confession of sin is acceptable to God. Motivation

distinguishes true from false confession. What drives you to confess sin? Are you sorry for the sin or just sorry for the negative consequences that sin produces? Tim Keller comments:

> *You may admit your sin, but you aren't really sorry for the sin itself. You are sorry about the painful consequences to you. You want that pain to stop, so you end the behavior. It may be, however, that there hasn't been any real inward alteration of the false beliefs and hopes, the inordinate desires, and the mistaken self-perceptions that caused the sin.*[1]

Many confess – agreeing with God concerning their sin – yet stop short of more fully dealing with it. In his classic work, *The Mortification of Sin*, Puritan theologian, John Owen, echoes this thought:

> *It is evident that thou contendest against* **sin** *merely because of thy own* **trouble** *by it. Would thy conscience be quiet under it, thou wouldst let it alone.*[2]

REPENTANCE

Confession often fails to stop future sin simply because true repentance does not occur. "To repent" literally means to "turn around," as in you are going one direction and make a 180 degree turn to go the other direction.. John Stott said that real repentance is characterized not only by admitting or confessing sin, but by forsaking it.[3] We might compare this to someone admitting they robbed a bank (confession), but who continues to rob banks in the future, instead of forsaking that practice. John Owen put it this way:

> *If ever thou wilt mortify thy corruptions, thou must tie up thy conscience to the law, shut it from all shifts and exceptions, until it owns its guilt with a clear and thorough apprehension . . . Bring thy lust to the gospel – not for relief, but for farther conviction of its guilt; look on Him whom thou hast pierced, and be in bitterness. Say to thy soul, "What have I done? What love, what mercy, what blood, what grace have I despised and trampled on! Is this the return I make to the Father for his love, to the Son for his blood, to the Holy Ghost for his grace? Do I thus requite the Lord? Have I defiled the heart that Christ died to wash, that the blessed Spirit hath chosen to dwell in?*[4]

Owen emphasized contemplating the majesty and grace of God as the key principle in killing (mortifying) sin. The issue is not that we have made a mistake or damaged our life in some way, but rather that we have offended the Holy One who loves us and died for us:

> *Be much in thoughtfulness of the excellency of the majesty of God and thine infinite, inconceivable distance from him. Many thought of it cannot but fill thee with a sense of thine own vileness, which strikes deep at the root of any indwelling sin.*[5]

> *Will not a due apprehension of this inconceivable greatness of God, and that infinite distance wherein we stand from him fill the soul with a holy and awful fear of him, so as to keep it in a frame unsuited to the thriving or flourishing of any lust whatever?*[6]

If confession is only "admitting" we have sinned without deep contrition and humiliation, it accomplishes little other than rubbing a salve on our conscience only to see it quickly dissipate. God would deeply touch us and change us through our sin experiences. A casual contemplation of our sin will not bring lasting change. However, genuine repentance is a gift of God, developed in the believer anchored in an understanding of who God is and what he has done for them.

CONFESSION EXEMPLIFIED – SAUL

Scripture provides both good and bad examples of confession. Saul is a bad example. The prophet, Samuel, delivered God's order that Saul was to utterly destroy the Amalekites. However Saul spared the king and the best of the spoil. He essentially saved the "good stuff" and destroyed that which was worthless (I Samuel 15:9). Samuel eventually arrives to hear Saul claim obedience to God's command:

> *I have performed the commandment of the LORD* (I Samuel 15:13)

Samuel, of course, wasn't buying this and replied:

> *What then is this bleating of the sheep in my ears and the lowing of the oxen that I hear?* (v. 14)

Saul has his concocted story and is sticking to it. He again denies his disobedience and goes further to blame the people for sparing the choice animals and then to justify that behavior proposing it had a godly purpose:

> *I have obeyed the voice of the LORD. I have gone on the mission on which the LORD sent me. I have brought Agag the king of Amalek, and I have devoted the Amalekites to destruction. But the people took of the spoil, sheep and oxen, the best of the things devoted to destruction, to sacrifice to the LORD your God in Gilgal.* (v. 20-21)

Try as hard as he might, Saul cannot weasel out of the clear fact that he sinned against God by disobeying a clear command. After yet another rebuke by Samuel, he inadequately confesses:

> *Saul said to Samuel, "I have sinned, for I have transgressed the commandment of the LORD and your words, because I feared the people and obeyed their voice. Now therefore, please pardon my sin and return with me that I may bow before the LORD."* (v. 24-25)

Saul's confession contained neither godly sorrow nor real repentance. His only sorrow was how all of this would adversely affect him. We know that from his next statement to Samuel, requesting that he not make his sin known to the people:

> *Then he said, "I have sinned; yet honor me now before the elders of my people and before Israel, and return with me, that I may bow before the LORD your God."* (v. 30)

It's all wrapped up in "I have sinned, yet honor me." Saul was concerned, not with God's honor, but with his own. He cares not that God was offended, even referring to "the LORD your God," rather than claiming a relationship with God for himself. His confession is utterly self-centered and contains no genuine repentance. What a difference it would have made had he acknowledged and forsook his sin rather than justifying it! His false confession took his life on a downward spiral ending in a humiliating defeat and death.

CONFESSION EXEMPLIFIED – DAVID

By contrast, David presents a wonderful example of biblical confession and repentance. David also sinned, in his case by committing adultery with Bathsheba and then murdering her husband to cover it up. Like Saul, David is confronted with his sin by another of God's prophets – Nathan – by way of a story about a stolen lamb. Upon Nathan's conclusion that, "You are the man!" (II Samuel 12:7), David immediately confesses, "I have sinned against the LORD" (v. 13). With David, unlike Saul, there is no "yet" or "but" – he fully owns responsibility for his sin. Even more than that, David saw his sin as "against the LORD," while Saul failed to grasp that important distinction. The details of David's confession of sin are revealed in Psalm 51:1-12:

> *To the choirmaster. A Psalm of David, when Nathan the prophet went to him, after he had gone in to Bathsheba.*
> *Have mercy on me, O God, according to your steadfast love; according to your abundant mercy blot out my transgressions. Wash me thoroughly from my iniquity, and cleanse me from my sin! For I know my transgressions, and my sin is ever before me. Against you, you only, have I sinned and done what is evil in your sight, so that you may be justified in your words and blameless in your judgment. Behold, I was brought forth in iniquity, and in sin did my mother conceive me. Behold, you delight in truth in the inward being, and you teach me wisdom in the secret heart. Purge me with hyssop, and I shall be clean; wash me, and I shall be whiter than snow. Let me hear joy and gladness; let the bones that you have broken rejoice. Hide your face from my sins, and blot out all my iniquities. Create in me a clean heart, O God, and renew a right spirit within me. Cast me not away from your presence, and take not your Holy Spirit from me. Restore to me the joy of your salvation, and uphold me with a willing spirit.*

Here we see what genuine confession of sin looks like. We see a broken man, desperately appealing for the mercy of God. He comes with no excuses or blame of others. While the personal consequences of his sin are enormous, given the child of his illicit union will die, David focuses on his offense against God, to whom he pleads for cleansing and restoring purity to his heart.

You don't have to commit adultery and murder to identify with David's contrition, for "all have sinned and come short of the glory of God" (Romans 3:23). The more we truly see who God is, the more we see our own unworthiness. Thus, confession stands as an integral part of prayer. If we meditate at all on God and his word, we cannot fail to comprehend our own vileness before the Holy One. Confession is so much more than simple admission of our sin. It also encompasses the repenting and forsaking of that sin, but not in a fleshly "I'll try harder" approach. The power for repentance is also the gift of God's grace as we draw closer to him in prayer and meditation. With our heart thus properly prepared, we are ready to move into where most Christians spend their prayer time – petition.

APPLICATION & IMPLEMENTATION

1. Begin by praising God, meditating upon scripture that proclaims who God is and what he is like. Do you find yourself then motivated to confess sin?

2. After beginning your prayer time in praise and meditation, add confession of sin before making any petitions. Does that change anything concerning the petitions you present?

THIS CHAPTER IN A NUTSHELL

1. Confession is not to get forgiveness but to experience forgiveness.

2. Genuine confession involves not only admitting sin, but also forsaking it.

3. Confession should be motivated by the realization that we have offended God.

4. Saul and David provide negative and positive examples, respectively, of what confession should look like.

FOOTNOTES:

1. Keller, Timothy, Prayer: Experiencing Awe and Intimacy with God, (New York: Penguin Books, 2014), p. 213.

2. Owen, John, The Mortification of Sin, (fig-books.com, First Electronic Edition: January 2012), Location 740.

3. Stott, John R. W., Confess Your Sins: The Way of Reconciliation, (Word Books, 1974), p. 20.

4. Owen, Location 1058.

5. Ibid., Location 1150.

6. Ibid., Location 1288.

Chapter 7

Radical Petition

The function of prayer is not to influence God, but rather to change the nature of the one who prays. – Soren Kierkegaard

For most Christians, prayer is asking for stuff. We may give lip service to thanksgiving, praise and meditation, but the word "prayer" immediately suggests petitioning God for our perceived needs. Thus far we've seen that most biblical prayer is *not* petition, though petition is definitely legitimate and even commanded in scripture. The simple truth is that most of us need to up the praise and meditation and drastically reduce the petition aspects of our prayer life. However, the bigger issue is whether we are petitioning God for valid things – most believers do not.

MOTIVATION FOR PETITION

Why is it that most of our prayers revolve around petition? I believe we are driven by doubt of God's providential care. Do you really believe God is taking care of you? Or does anxiety more often creep in giving you that, "Where are you, God?" feeling? We really like to remind God, "Now don't you forget about me . . . I'm still here and I'm hurting!"

An obsession with petition demonstrates not only faithlessness, but a lack of intimacy with God. The more we praise God, the less we feel the need to petition him, for praise hammers into our minds the greatness of God's love, grace and mercy toward us. If we are truly experiencing an intimate relationship with God, we know our needs will be met. How obsessed (or not obsessed) we are with petitioning God measures how secure we are in that relationship.

JESUS' REBUKE

Christ clearly rebuked this obsessive petitioning in the Sermon on the

Mount:

> *And when you pray, do not heap up empty phrases as the Gentiles do, for they think that they will be heard for their many words. Do not be like them, for your Father knows what you need before you ask him.* (Matthew 6:7-8)

> *Therefore do not be anxious, saying, "What shall we eat?" or "What shall we drink?" or "What shall we wear?" For the Gentiles seek after all these things, and your heavenly Father knows that you need them all. But seek first the kingdom of God and his righteousness, and all these things will be added to you.* (Matthew 6:31-33)

This principle is perhaps best illustrated in our relationship with our own children. Do your children ask (i. e. "petition") you for every need that comes to their minds? Are they constantly asking you:

> *Don't forget to buy groceries!*
> *Please pay the utility bill!*
> *Did you lock the door?*
> *Be sure to drive carefully!*

If they did that, you would question their mental health or maybe wonder if they suffered from obsessive compulsive disorder (OCD). So why don't they constantly pepper you with these questions? It's simple: They know by experience that you are taking care of them. They presume their basic needs are provided. But where does that presumption come from? It comes from having an intimate relationship, which is what Jesus said in Matthew 6:32. We would shudder at the thought as imperfect parents that we needed to be reminded to put food on the table for our children, and yet we question whether our perfect heavenly Father will do that for us apart from our obsessive reminders. Our actions often suggest that we don't think God loves us as much as we love our own children. God forgive us for our utter blasphemy!

PRAYING OR WISHING?

Let me be blunt: The petitions most of us pray are not really praying – they are *wishing*. They express, not God's decreed, sovereign will, but our desires. We *wish* someone would be healed. We *wish* to have a safe trip. We *wish* to find a job. We *wish* to have a certain financial provision. We *wish* to find a spouse. We *wish* that some friend or relative would come to faith in Christ. These are all wishes – they are sentiments expressing how we feel.

So what's wrong with any of these petitions? They all seem like "good" things to us that would be most desirable. While that is true, these petitions all have a fundamental flaw:

You have no idea if any of these is the will of God

Yes, they are definitely your will, but you have no definite basis for *knowing* they are God's will.

PETITION REQUIRES A BASIS

The fundamental question you must ask on every petition you would lay before God is:

Is there a basis for this request?

Imagine coming into a courtroom, standing before the judge and asking for something for which you have no legal basis. Would you not be quickly dismissed from the proceedings? I actually had this experience once in representing myself before a judge. I diligently studied the relevant law. I carefully organized my thoughts and argument. Because of that preparation I had strong confidence approaching the bench. Isn't it odd that we prepare to state the basis for our request before an earthly judge, but don't apply the same seriousness to presenting our pleas before the Judge of the universe?

I sometimes wonder if God is laughing or incensed at my presumption in attempting to enlist his aid in doing my will! This common presumption in prayer has often made me unable to pray with a group of Christians, but rather to simply remain in polite silence. I hear petitions that are offensive – not because they are evil, but simply because they have no biblical basis and are therefore presumptive. For example, a client after one of those supposed "we think we got it all" cancer surgeries, said to me, "Pray that my cancer won't return." Now think about that. What possible basis would I have for praying that prayer? It isn't a prayer – it's a wish, and a very understandable and heartfelt one at that. However, I don't know what God's will is in that situation, and therefore I can't pray confidently according to the will of God (I John 5:14-15) for that request.

DETERMINING A BASIS FOR PETITION

So how do you determine a basis for a prayer petition? I believe there are three possibilities:

1. Specific Promise – Is there a specific promise or statement of God's will in Scripture that applies? In our earlier chapter on God's will and prayer, I noted three verses in the New Testament that specifically say, "This is God's will for you." But there are many more passages that define God's will without saying those words. Later in this chapter I will list some of those. Your job is to study the Scripture as a lawyer would study statutes and case law before petitioning the judge. Your confidence and faith will soar as you stand on that firm ground in making your petitions. In his sermon "Prayer – the Forerunner of Mercy" Charles Spurgeon spoke of praying God's promises this way:

> *First, I enquire what the promise is. I turn to my Bible, and I seek to find the promise whereby the thing which I desire to seek is certified to me as being a thing which God is willing to give. Having enquired so far as that, I take that promise, and on my bended knees I enquire of God whether he will fulfill his own promise. I take to him his own word of covenant, and I say to him, "O Lord, wilt thou not fulfill it, and wilt thou not fulfill it now?" So that there, again, prayer is enquiry. After prayer I look out for the answer; I expect to be heard; and if I am not answered I pray again, and my repeated prayers are but fresh enquiries.*

2. God's Attributes – A more general, though just as appropriate, basis for petition, is appealing to the attributes of God. I referred earlier to the client that asked me to pray her cancer wouldn't return. Rather than pray that, I instead appealed to the mercy of God applied to her as his child. In his attribute of mercy our heavenly Father so often provides relief to our suffering. Yet I don't presume that because God is merciful that my time is his time for expressing that mercy. He is, after all, accomplishing far more objectives than I could ever imagine in the suffering of one of his children.

3. Leading of the Holy Spirit – The *distinct* leading of the Holy Spirit can reveal God's will to you in a given situation. God can impress upon you that it is his will to heal someone, to bring them to faith or to provide in some specific way. However, this requires great care, discernment and maturity. One can easily be deceived as to the Spirit's leading and become presumptive. You should not assume you are led of the Spirit regarding God's will without confirmation in scripture.

FLAWS IN COMMON PETITIONS

Let's look at the flaws in six of the most common petitions Christians pray:

1. Physical Healing – Perhaps the most common petition prayed is for physical healing, either for others or for ourselves. The fact of the matter is that we've all seen people die for whom we've prayed for healing. That alone tells us that it is not God's will to heal every physical disease.

However, that doesn't stop many alleged Christian teachers from proclaiming that God's will is to physically heal everyone, and if you're not healed, it's because you didn't have enough faith. I even know of one pastor who took this so far as to say that if he had enough faith, he wouldn't even physically die! That whole theology is a gross perversion of God's priorities. This very temporary, physical life is not the most important thing in God's eyes. Transforming us into the image of Christ *through* the experiences of this life is his priority (Romans 12:2, II Corinthians 3:18).

There are clearly times when God wills healing and directs us to pray for it, either privately or through the elders of the local church (James

5:14-16). Don't act presumptively, as if that healing is somehow a right or demand you can hold over God. Instead focus on how God so often works dramatically through illness. As C. S. Lewis notes in *The Problem of Pain*:

> *God whispers to us in our pleasures, speaks in our conscience, but shouts in our pain: it is His megaphone to rouse a deaf world.*

2. Travel Safety – Another very common prayer petition is for "traveling mercies" – to be kept safe on a trip. Does God actually promise to keep us safe every time we travel? Many Christians have been hurt or killed while traveling. Is that because they didn't first pray for traveling mercies? I recall being interviewed on a Christian TV network by a local pastor and his wife regarding one of my books. Sometime after that they were both killed in a plane crash returning from a vacation in Mexico, leaving a devastated teenage daughter. Was that because they failed to pray for safety? Of course not! Ultimately we just don't know God's purposes in all that he allows, but must trust him through the unexplained.

Praying for traveling safety is another example of wishing rather than praying. We desire not to be harmed, and understandably so. But what if God has some higher purpose in our being harmed? Do you wonder if the parents of the famous hymn writer, Fanny Crosby, pondered how God allowed their infant to become blind through medical malpractice? Yet had that not happened we probably wouldn't even know her name today. She would not have enriched the church with thousands of hymns borne out of her physically broken life. We would be wise to remember God's Word in Isaiah:

> *For my thoughts are not your thoughts, neither are your ways my ways, declares the LORD. For as the heavens are higher than the earth, so are my ways higher than your ways and my thoughts than your thoughts.* (Isaiah 55:8-9)

Shouldn't we first seek his will before presuming we need extra protection? We are totally safe in the context of God's purposes for our lives. We can rightly pray that nothing interfere with the fulfillment of his plan and design. I think that's the way we should look at passages like Psalm 91:

> *He who dwells in the shelter of the Most High will abide in the shadow of the Almighty. I will say to the LORD, "My refuge and my fortress, my God, in whom I trust." For he will deliver you from the snare of the fowler and from the deadly pestilence. He will cover you with his pinions, and under his wings you will find refuge; his faithfulness is a shield and buckler. You will not fear the terror of the night, nor the arrow that flies by day, nor the pestilence that stalks in darkness, nor the destruction that wastes at noon day. A thousand may fall at your side, ten thousand at your right hand, but it will not come near you.* (Psalm 91:1-7)

The key to understanding this often cited passage for protection lies in the first verse – "He who dwells in the shelter of the Most High . . ." God will keep you safe in the context of his purposes for you. No harm will touch you such that his purposes would be thwarted. However, should his purposes *not* require our protection and preservation, this promise doesn't really apply.

3. Employment – Prayers for employment in general can be legitimate in that God commands us to work (I Thessalonians 4:11-12; II Thessalonians 3:12). The problem comes in when you pray for a specific job. At that point you are wishing, not praying. Your petition for employment must express the desire to fulfill God's will and purposes with your employment, rather than asking God to fulfill your will and purposes. Always remember that delays and struggles are among his favorite tools to transform your life.

4. Financial Needs – Indeed there are promises related to provision, including financial provision:

> *And my God will supply every need of yours according to his riches in glory in Christ Jesus.* (Philippians 4:19)

But we also know that God works through poverty, indeed as he does in all manner of affliction:

> *. . . through many tribulations we must enter the kingdom of God.* (Acts 14:22b)

The question concerns God's will and timing. As you immerse yourself in his Word and meditate upon his attributes, his Spirit will enlighten and direct.

5. Spouse Provision – Scripture indicates that for most it is God's will to marry. Thus, there is a basis for praying for that provision or for God to reveal a calling to singleness. The trouble enters with the specifics, that is, praying that you might marry a particular person. You have no way of knowing if that person is God's choice, apart from a confirmed impression by the Holy Spirit. All else is presumption.

6. Salvation of Another Person – Is it legitimate to pray for an unbeliever's salvation? My answer is "yes" and "no," depending on certain factors. I'll cover this in detail in our next chapter concerning intercession.

MAKING BIBLICAL PETITIONS

The main goal of this book is to help Christians pray biblically. So how does one craft *biblical* petitions to present before God? The overriding principle is again the question:

Is there a basis for making this request?

Am I trying to line up with God's decreed will, or am I trying to enlist God to serve my desired will? Helga Bergold Gross, in one of the most famous quotes on prayer, said:

> *What we usually pray to God is not that His will be done, but that He approve ours.*

Alan Redpath captures the same sentiment in saying:

> *Before we can pray, "Lord, Thy Kingdom come," we must be willing to pray, "My Kingdom go."*

So my questions are simply these:

- Have you searched his Word to discern his will?
- Have you contemplated God's relevant attributes?
- Have you spent time just listening in his presence?

APPRECIATING THE PARADOX

Anyone who has studied the Bible's teachings on prayer has encountered a paradox regarding prayer. On the one hand, we recognize that we are coming before the Creator and Judge of the universe and thus would do well to heed Solomon's advice:

> *Be not rash with your mouth, nor let your heart be hasty to utter a word before God, for God is in heaven and you are on earth. Therefore let your words be few.* (Ecclesiastes 5:2)

On the other hand, in Christ we have the privilege of boldly approaching the throne of grace in prayer (Hebrews 4:16). Further, we are told to pray about everything (Philippians 4:6) and to pray without ceasing (I Thessalonians 5:17).

So how do we handle the paradox? We simply must always tremble at the majesty and holiness of God, yet also rejoice that through the blood of Christ we are able to confidently approach him as Abba, Father. We approach him based, not on our merit, but solely on the merit of Christ.

WHAT SHOULD I PETITION GOD FOR?

Enough of what we should *not* pray for. Let's turn to the positive and what our petitions *should* be. Before listing some examples, though, I must again emphasize that the focus of our prayers should *not* be on petition. First practice praise, meditation, confession and thanksgiving, leaving petition as the least activity in prayer.

So how do you figure out the legitimate petitions – the ones that have a basis? It's pretty simple really – just read the Bible and take note. I started in Matthew and proceeded through the epistles finding the following legitimate petitions:

1. For those who persecute you (Matthew 5:44)
2. For the fulfillment of God's kingdom (Matthew 6:10)
3. For God's will to be done (Matthew 6:10)
4. For daily physical provision (Matthew 6:11)
5. For protection from temptation (Matthew 6:13; Luke 22:40, 46)
6. For those who mistreat you (Luke 6:28)
7. For workers to be sent into the spiritual harvest (Luke 10:2)
8. For forgiveness (Matthew 6:12; Acts 8:22)
9. For believers' restoration (II Corinthians 13:9)
10. For growing love with knowledge and discernment (Philippians 1:9)
11. For knowledge of God's will (Colossians 1:9)
12. For spiritual wisdom and understanding (Colossians 1:9)
13. To walk in a manner worthy of the Lord (Colossians 1:10)
14. To be fully pleasing to God (Colossians 1:10)
15. To bear fruit in good works (Colossians 1:10)
16. To increase in your knowledge of God (Colossians 1:10)
17. To be strengthened with God's power (Colossians 1:11)
18. For endurance and patience with joy (Colossians 1:11)
19. To give thanks to the Father for redemption (Colossians 1:12)
20. For sanctification in body, mind and spirit (I Thessalonians 5:23)
21. That God would make you worthy of his calling (II Thessalonians 1:11)
22. That God would fulfill every resolve for good (II Thessalonians 1:11)
23. That God would fulfill every work of faith with power (II Thessalonians 1:11)
24. That the Word of the Lord would speed ahead and be honored (II Thessalonians 3:1)
25. Pray if suffering (James 5:13)
26. Pray for healing (James 5:14)
27. Pray for health and prosperity (3 John 2)

I'm sure this is a very incomplete list from just the New Testament, but let me ask the question: Is this enough for you to pray for? I'm convinced any believer could keep quite busy just praying for the above twenty-seven biblical petitions. Moreover, when you pray for the above, you can absolutely **know** you are praying the will of God. That will produce faith and enable you to pray **believing** and be assured of God's affirmative answer.

WHAT IS "ANSWERED PRAYER?"

No discussion of petitionary prayer would be complete without also defining what an answer to prayer is. A good way to assess the quality of your petition prayers is to ask what percentage of your petitions get answered? If you are honest, and if you know what a "yes" answer is biblically speaking, it's probably going to be 10 or 20 percent at best.
Now don't come back with the popular Christian cliche' that all your prayers are answered – some are answered "yes," some are answered "no," and some are answered "later." That may sound cute, but it's not at all biblical. How we love to "cover" for God and give him a way out of not being to blame for our unanswered prayers! Frankly, that old line is just a cop out for a disappointing prayer life. Now let me prove my point biblically. In John 15:7 we read:

> *If you abide in me, and my words abide in you, ask whatever you wish, and it will be done for you.*

The answer to prayer is clearly a "yes." If you ask whatever you wish, but it is not done for you, could you possibly justify that "no" answer with this passage? No way! How about Matthew 21:22:

> *And whatever you ask in prayer, you will receive, if you have faith.*

Again, could "no" be considered consistent with this passage? It clearly contemplates receiving the thing asked for – a "yes" answer. Then there's James 5:13-15:

> *Is anyone among you suffering? Let him pray. Is anyone cheerful? Let him sing praise. Is anyone among you sick? Let*

> *him call for the elders of the church, and let them pray over him, anointing him with oil in the name of the Lord. And the prayer of faith will save the one who is sick, and the Lord will raise him up. And if he has committed sins, he will be forgiven.*

Will you tell me that the person not being healed is still an "answer" to the prayer described? I don't think so. Or, how about Psalm 34:4:

> *I sought the LORD, and he answered me and delivered me from all my fears.*

The "answer" was being delivered from fear. Not being delivered from fear would constitute no answer to the prayer. Similarly we can see in scripture that not getting your petition is a "no" answer. Take II Corinthians 12:8-9a:

> *Three times I pleaded with the Lord about this, that it should leave me. But he said to me, "My grace is sufficient for you, for my power is made perfect in weakness."*

Paul would consider his prayer answered if the thorn in the flesh were removed, but it wasn't. God did, however, tell him why he was not answering his petition. Another famous example is found in Matthew 26:39, 42:

> *And going a little farther he fell on his face and prayed, saying, "My Father, if it be possible, let this cup pass from me; nevertheless, not as I will, but as you will." . . . Again a second time, he went away and prayed, "My Father, if this cannot pass unless I drink it, your will be done."*

This is another unanswered prayer in that the petition was denied – fortunately for us! Jesus clearly understood that his prayer was not to be answered due to the will of God for something greater.

I don't want to harp on this too much, but understand that we don't have to tie ourselves in knots to justify a prayer life that isn't really working. When it comes to a petition for something, an answer means a "yes." A "no" or a "later" is not an answer, biblically speaking.

THE REASON FOR UNANSWERED PRAYER

Now that we've defined what an answered petition prayer is, why you think most of your prayers don't get answered? As we covered in earlier chapters: **You were praying your will, not God's will.** It's really that simple. Our will is nothing; his will is everything. Your prayer life will change dramatically when you pray according to God's will. You will know things will happen, you will have faith in your prayers being answered, and prayer will get really exciting. But there is still more to say about petition. There is a way to biblically order and present your petitions to God. That's next.

APPLICATION & IMPLEMENTATION

1. For several days take your prayers of petition for yourself or others from Colossians 1:9-12. Observe how that changes your prayer experience.

2. Based on Colossians 1:9 ask God to show you if a particular prayer petition is his will and wait for his answer through his Word and Spirit.

THIS CHAPTER IN A NUTSHELL

1. To most Christians prayer means petition – asking for stuff.

2. With increasing intimacy with God, obsession with petition decreases.

3. Most prayers of petition are "wishing" rather than true praying.

4. Prayer petitions require a basis in God's promises, attributes or Spirit leading.

5. The Scriptures define numerous legitimate petitions to bring to God.

6. An "answered" prayer is one in which God grants your request.

Chapter 8

Radical Order & Argument

I would lay my case before him and fill my mouth with arguments. (Job 23:4)

"Monte Kline, Defendant Pro Se." Those were my opening words after the Superior Court judge took her seat. It was a simple hearing in a multi-year legal battle over health freedom—a battle I later got an award from a national organization for fighting. My snooty Harvard lawyer didn't want to bother with it, so I chose to represent myself (and save a thousand dollars to boot). I was organized and prepared to the nth degree. I knew the law, as well as the judge's ruling I was challenging. There was a lot at stake – if it went the wrong way I faced a 100% shutdown of my business. I was totally confident and mostly prevailed in the hearing.

So why am I telling this courtroom story of many years ago? To understand prayer, you have to understand courtroom proceedings. Did you know that "prayer" is actually a legal term? The law.com dictionary defines "prayer" this way:

> *n. the specific request for judgment, relief and/or damages at the conclusion of a complaint or petition . . . A prayer gives the judge an idea of what is sought, and may become the basis of a judgment if the defendant defaults.*

Every time you pray a petition you come before the Judge making a case.

ARGUING WITH GOD?

In petitionary prayer you come to make an argument before God. This is not an argument in the sense of hostility or any sense of superiority, but rather an argument based upon God's word, promises and character. Charles Spurgeon brilliantly captured this concept in a sermon entitled "Order & Argument in Prayer" given

July 15, 1866 at the Metropolitan Tabernacle in London. This chapter is largely based upon that amazing sermon to which I can hopefully do justice. This concept will transform you prayers of petition more than anything I know of.

COMING BEFORE THE JUDGE

How seriously do you regard prayer? I know you think it's really important and that it is an amazing privilege, but how do you approach God? Do you come to him casually or gripped by his awesomeness? Do you come to him prepared to lay out your case, or do you just blabber out whatever comes to mind? In my story above, how would that judge have responded had I come to court with a casual, unprepared attitude?

We do have a paradox in approaching God, as I referred to in the previous chapter. God is different than an earthly judge in that he is both transcendent and immanent. He is infinitely distant from us in his holy and exalted state. He is the Judge of the Universe, and yet he is also "Abba, Father" whom we may **boldly** approach with our needs (Hebrews 4:16). But we must not lose our sense of awe when we come into his presence. Spurgeon describes this as "ordering our prayer:"

> *The ancient saints were wont, with Job, to order their cause before God; that is to say, as a petitioner coming into Court does not come there without thought to state his case on the spur of the moment, but enters into the audience chamber with his suit well prepared, having moreover learned how he ought to behave himself in the presence of the great One to whom he is appealing. In times of distress we may fly to God just as we are, as the dove enters the cleft of the rock, even though her plumes are ruffled; but in ordinary times we should not come with an unprepared spirit, even as a child comes not to his father in the morning till he has washed his face . . . God forbid that our prayer should be a mere leaping out of one's bed and kneeling down, and saying anything that comes first to hand; on the contrary, may we wait upon the Lord with holy fear and sacred awe.*

PREPARING OUR HEART

It is common in our day for Christians to *arrange* their prayer life around the acrostic A.C.T.S. – Adoration, Confession, Thanksgiving and Supplication. Spurgeon was very critical of prayer "arrangements," saying "It is no mere mechanical order I have been referring to," noting:

> *The true spiritual order of prayer seems to me to consist in something more than mere arrangement. It is most fitting for us first to feel that we are now doing something that is real; that we are about to address ourselves to God, Whom we cannot see, but Who is really present; Whom we can neither touch nor hear, nor by our senses can apprehend, but Who, nevertheless, is as truly with us as though we were speaking to a friend of flesh and blood like ourselves. Feeling the reality God's presence, our mind will be led by divine grace into a humble state; we shall feel like Abraham, when he said, "I have taken upon myself to speak unto God, I that am but dust and ashes." Consequently we shall not deliver matter of rote, much less shall we speak as if we were rabbis instructing our pupils, or as I have heard some do, with the coarseness of a highwayman stopping a person on the road and demanding his purse of him; but we shall be humble yet bold petitioners, humbly importuning mercy through the Saviour's blood. When I feel that I am in the presence of God, and take my rightful position in that presence, the next thing I shall want to recognize will be that I have no right to what I am seeking, and cannot expect to obtain it except as a gift of grace, and I must recollect that God limits the channel through which He will give me mercy – He will give it to me through His dear Son. Let me put myself then under the patronage of the great Redeemer. Let me feel that now it is no longer I that speak but Christ that speaketh with me, and that while I plead, I plead His wounds, His life, His death, His blood, Himself. This is truly getting into order.*

You won't radically transform your prayer life by finding the right "formula" or method. Learn to shun mere mechanical formulas as you understand that right prayer starts with a right heart.

ARGUMENTS IN PRAYER

When I say "arguments in prayer" do you cringe a little? Though that's a typical first reaction, understand this doesn't mean challenging God, but rather aligning our petition with God. Why does the concept of "argument" even enter in? Spurgeon notes:

> *Why are arguments to be used at all? is the first enquiry; the reply being, Certainly not because God is slow to give, nor because we can change the divine purpose, nor because God needeth to be informed of any circumstance with regard to ourselves or of anything in connection with the mercy asked: the arguments to be used are for our own benefit not for his. He requires for us to plead with Him, and to bring forth our strong reasons, as Isaiah saith,* **because this will show that we feel the value of the mercy** [emphasis added] . . . *If God's mercies came to us unasked, they would not be half so useful as they now are, when they have to be sought for; for now we get a double blessing, a blessing in the obtaining, and a blessing in the seeking.*

God actually *requires* us to present an argument with our petitions. That's how we grow and thus are blessed. Back to our courtroom illustration, have you ever heard of a judge just deciding a case without first hearing the arguments? Ever require your children to ask for something they want – to make a "case" for it before you grant it? Why not just give them everything they want without a justifying request? You don't do that because it wouldn't be good for their growing to maturity. God is certainly no less caring.

Let's now look at the actual process you may go through in arguing a petition before God. This takes time and effort and study, just as it would for a lawyer preparing a brief to present before a judge. But it will transform your experience of petitionary prayer.

STEP ONE – ARGUING GOD'S ATTRIBUTES

Take a look at the prayers in the Bible, such as in the Psalms, and note how often they focus on God's attributes – mercy, grace, justice, love and the like. For example, in Psalm 99:1-5 we read:

> *The LORD reigns; let the peoples tremble! He sits enthroned upon the cherubim; let the earth quake! The LORD is great in Zion; he is exalted over all the peoples. Let them praise your great and awesome name! Holy is he! The King in his might loves justice. You have*

> *established equity; you have executed justice and righteousness in Jacob. Exalt the LORD our God; worship at his footstool! Holy is he!*

Your prayers of petition are totally dependent upon the character of the One to whom you are praying. Thus, it is supremely important to make your appeal based upon God's attributes. In his sermon Spurgeon put it this way:

> *So you and I may take hold at any time upon the justice, the mercy, the faithfulness, the wisdom, the long-suffering, the tenderness of God, and we shall find every attributes of the Most High to be, as it were, a great battering-ram, with which we may open the gates of heaven.*

Ask yourself what attributes of God favor your petition and then dig into the Bible to document them, essentially as your "case law."

For example, let's say you are petitioning God regarding a health problem. What attributes of God would help make your case? How about his love? I don't think so, given his love often requires the chastening of suffering, as noted in Hebrews 12:6. Surely there is no relief in God's omniscience or omnipresence. How about his justice? No way! As rebellious children of Adam's fallen race justice would only require more suffering. The key attribute to "bring before the bar" would most likely be his mercy. So then you would take a concordance or topical Bible and search the Scripture for statements of God's mercy. Become fully immersed in that attribute and plead it in your petition. State those attribute defining scriptures before God in prayer.

STEP TWO – ARGUING GOD'S PROMISES

Are your petitions linked to the promises of God? If God hasn't spoken by way of an applicable promise, why are you asking in the first place? Without a promise from God as the foundation of your petition, you are really just "wishing" instead of praying. In my encounter with the judge, mere "wishing" for a favorable decision would not suffice. I had to have a basis for making my claim. In prayer, a promise from God is solid ground upon which to stand and have full assurance, as Spurgeon preached:

> *My brother, if you have a divine promise, you need not plead that with an "if" in it; you may plead with a certainty. If for the mercy which you are now asking, you have God's solemnly pledged word, there will scarce be any room for the caution about submission to His will. You know His will: that will is in the promise; plead it. Do not give Him rest until He fulfill it. He meant to fulfill it, or else He would not have given it.*

Obviously, this again requires work and time and study to ferret out relevant promises from the Bible. But the confidence you gain from standing on those promises will be well worth the effort.

STEP THREE – ARGUING GOD'S NAME

When you present a prayer petition to God, how concerned are you with the impact of that petition on God's reputation? Do you ever ask yourself, "What will unbelievers think of God if he does not grant my petition?" If you're like me, your focus is not on how it affects God's reputation, but how it affects your own. Yet biblical example shows us that successful intercession cares very much about God's reputation, as previously referred to with Moses' intercession for Israel:

> *But Moses implored the Lord his God and said, "O Lord, why does your wrath burn hot against your people, whom you have brought out of the land of Egypt with great power and with a mighty hand? Why should the Egyptians say, 'With evil intent did he bring them out, to kill them in the mountains and to consume them from the face of the earth'? Turn from your burning anger and relent of this disaster against your people.* (Exodus 32:11-12)

This can be a difficult argument to formulate. With certain petitions you may struggle to find a relevant basis. However, a non-response to most any petition from one of his children potentially may lead an observing unbeliever to defame the name of God. Perhaps the greatest benefit of offering this argument is simply getting our focus on God and off of ourselves.

STEP FOUR – ARGUING THE SORROWS OF GOD'S PEOPLE

God has great compassion, love and mercy for his children. He feels our pain, as captured in the lyrics of the Casting Crowns song "Praise You in This Storm:"

> *Every tear I've cried, you hold in your hand.*

This is the repeated message of scripture:

> *Hear my prayer, O LORD, and give ear to my cry; hold not your peace at my tears!* (Psalm 39:12)
>
> *You have kept count of my tossings; put my tears in your bottle. Are they not in your book?* (Psalm 56:8)
>
> *The LORD is near to the brokenhearted and saves the crushed in spirit.* (Psalm 34:18)
>
> *I dwell in the high and holy place, and also with him who is of a contrite and lowly spirit, to revive the spirit of the lowly, and to revive the heart of the contrite.* (Isaiah 57:15b)
>
> *Go and say to Hezekiah, Thus says the LORD, the God of David your father: I have heard your prayer; I have seen your tears. Behold, I will add fifteen years to your life.* (Isaiah 38:5)
>
> *He will wipe away every tear from their eyes, and death shall be no more, neither shall there be mourning nor crying nor pain anymore, for the former things have passed away.* (Revelation 21:4)

In these and other similar passages we see the tender heart of God toward his children. Charles Spurgeon remarks:

> *Nothing is so eloquent with the father as his child's cry; yes, there is one thing more mighty still, and that is a moan – when the child is so sick that it is past crying, and lies moaning with that kind of moan which indicates extreme suffering and intense weakness. Who can resist that*

moan?

In certain situations this is an appropriate appeal, especially after long, exhausting suffering. God will only continue to allow suffering in his children if it serves his purposes and is for our ultimate good (Romans 8:28). We know neither the full design of our sufferings nor their timing, but nevertheless this is a legitimate appeal to consider.

STEP FIVE – ARGUING GOD'S PAST PROVISIONS

Have you ever noticed how often God's past work is recalled in the Scripture, particularly in the Old Testament? The key word here is **remember**:

> *Seek the LORD and his strength; seek his presence continually! Remember the wondrous works that he has done, his miracles and the judgment he uttered, O offspring of Israel his servant, sons of Jacob, his chosen ones!* (I Chronicles 16:11-13)

This idea is repeated in Psalm 105, which has a "remember God's past works" theme.

You may think about this in two ways: Past provisions in scripture and past provisions in your own life. You may recall before God story after story from the Bible as to his provisions for his people from Adam through the Apostles. But you also have your own story of God's working. Recall before him how he has provided for your needs in the past, the logic being: "God, I witnessed time and again throughout my life how you have provided for my needs. I trust you to again do that." Spurgeon comments:

> *Brethren, we have to deal with an unchanging God, who will do in the future what He has done in the past, because He never turns from His purpose, and cannot be thwarted in His design; the past thus becomes a very mighty means of winning blessings from Him.*

STEP SIX – ARGUING THE SUFFERINGS, DEATH, MERIT AND INTERCESSION OF CHRIST

Spurgeon called this the grand Christian argument to place before the throne of God:

> *Brethren, I am afraid we do not understand what it is that we have at our command when we are allowed to plead with God for Christ's sake . . . Supposing you should say to me, you who keep a warehouse in the city, "Sir, call at my office, and use my name, and say that they are to give you such a thing." I should go in and use your name, and I should obtain my request as a matter of right and a matter of necessity. This is virtually what Jesus Christ says to us, "If you need anything of God, all that the Father has belongs to me; go and use my name . . . When thou pleadest the name of Christ thou pleadest that which shakes the gates of hell, and which the hosts of heaven obey, and God Himself feels the sacred power of that divine plea.*

This is your greatest appeal. This is what it means to pray "in Jesus' name." It's not tacking "In Jesus' Name" on the end of your prayers (though that's okay if you really know what it means), but something truly profound. It means you are approaching God, not on your own and not as yourself, but clothed and covered by the suffering, death, merit and intercession of Christ. On our own we have nothing to claim as we come before God, but coming in Christ we have claim to anything Christ has before the Father.

I fondly remember an illustration the late Pastor Ron Dunn of Dallas gave early in my Christian ministry of this concept. He had taken his kids to a carnival and bought a bunch of tickets for them to go on rides. The kids would line up in front of him and he would tear off a ticket for each one until he saw a boy he had never seen in his life with his hand out! He immediately withheld giving the boy a ticket until his son said, "It's okay Dad; he's my friend." On that word from his son Pastor Dunn immediately tore off a ticket and gave it to that stranger – *in the name of his son.* We are that strange child with our hand out to the Father with no right to his provision until the Son says, "Father, he is my friend. Grant his request in my name."

IMPLEMENTATION

Spurgeon's "Order and Argument in Prayer" is profoundly powerful, but it's only theoretical until you actually do it. So, here's the how-to:

1. When you have a significant petition to bring to God, prepare – order it. Consider seriously who you are coming before. Think it through versus just blurting something out. Prepare your heart.
2. Sit down, preferably with your journal, and write your prayer petition using the six arguments. This will require some time and Bible study. It usually takes me at least two hours to go through this process. I know that writing prayers is not fashionable these days since many think this somehow quenches genuineness and spontaneity. I would reply that it's actually better, in that you have a real basis for your prayer and therefore you can get excited about it and truly pray believing and expecting God to act.

If you're not willing to spend an hour or two developing your prayer argument, it's not because this is an inferior method of prayer. Let's be honest: It's because of laziness. This is work! This requires you to dig in deep in the Scriptures *before* you pray. But do this work, and you will stand on solid ground. You will actually be praying instead of wishing. I dare you to try it.

APPLICATION & IMPLEMENTATION

1. Imagine you had to make a case before an earthly judge. What preparation would you likely do? How would you conduct yourself? What would be your expectation?

2. With your greatest prayer need in mind, write out a prayer based upon the six "arguments" Spurgeon lists. Then pray that prayer until it is either answered or you are directed to alter it.

THIS CHAPTER IN A NUTSHELL

1. To understand petitionary prayer, we must understand

coming before a judge in a courtroom.

2. Preparation for petitioning God requires ordering our prayer.

3. In prayer we present arguments as a basis for God granting our request.

4. In petitioning God we argue his attributes, promises, name, sorrows of his people, past provisions and the work of Christ on our behalf.

5. Writing out a prayer with the six arguments, after thorough study, generates faith and assurance in an affirmative answer.

Chapter 9

Radical Intercession

First of all, I urge that supplications, prayer, intercessions, and thanksgiving be made for all people . . . (I Timothy 2:1)

"Please pray that my cancer won't return." As shared in the previous chapter, these were the words I heard from a client requesting intercessory prayer on her behalf. Undoubtedly you have heard many similar requests, given that intercession is perhaps the most common form of prayer practiced today. As we will discover, intercession is also the most misused type of prayer.

Intercession is simply petitionary prayer for others, but like other prayer petitions, we must first ask:

Is there a basis for the prayer request?

Though we can pray *for* everyone who asks, we should not pray for *anything* someone asks. Our responsibility is to first maintain a submission to God's will and Word. That fidelity dictates what it is and is not appropriate to intercede for.

INTERCESSION RIGHT AND WRONG

There is a right and a wrong way to intercede depending on your view of God. The wrong way is in trying to persuade God to change his mind about something. God is immutable, that is unchangeable. We read in Malachi 4:6:

> *For I the LORD do not change.*

When you intercede you are not giving God new information, for he is also omniscient. Further, in intercession you are not overcoming God's reluctance to do something, for he is righteous and good. Overall, the error we most often make about God is summarized in Psalm 50:21:

You thought that I was one like yourself.

We change our minds, so we approach God as if he does as well. We get new information about the situations affecting us, so we assume God is like us. We are reluctant to do certain things, but we do respond to persuasion, so we project that value upon God. These grievous errors not only thwart any meaningful intercessory prayer life, but also preclude basic Christian maturity.

INTERCEDING THE RIGHT WAY

So, how do we correctly intercede in prayer? First, we recognize that God wrote the story, and that he wrote it not only before we were born, but before the creation. He doesn't merely know the end of the story out of his omniscience, but he is the writer, producer and director of the story. He is not sitting back waiting to be persuaded to act. Most importantly, we were chosen to play a part in his story, including practicing intercessory prayer.

Correct intercession requires so much more than empathy with the needs of others – it requires first an intimate connection with God. As an intercessor you must be one who discerns his will through his Word, his promises and his attributes. Further, you must become attuned to the heart of God, being broken over what breaks his heart and willing to minister his desires on behalf of others.

EXAMPLES OF INTERCESSION

Whole books could be written on the examples of intercession found in the Bible, but I will only mention a few:

Abraham over Sodom – This Bible story from Genesis 18 is often presented to suggest that God really does "change his mind" in response to human intercession. During his angelic visitation, God tells Abraham that he is going to visit Sodom to evaluate the situation there. Abraham then proceeds to "negotiate" with God that he would not destroy the city if fifty, then forty-five, then forty, then thirty, then twenty, then ten righteous were found there. Of course, not even ten righteous people were found there, so it was destroyed.

If you believe God really changed his mind in this instance, you also must believe that God had to physically visit Sodom to find out what was going on there – in other words, that God was not omniscient (and therefore not God). This passage is a classic example of **anthropomorphism** in Scripture, that is, the attributing of human characteristics to God in order to communicate on our level. The totality of scripture makes it quite clear that God has indeed decreed everything that comes to pass and that he is omniscient. The key point is that God decreed **both** the fate of Sodom and Abraham's intercession – both were part of his story from before time began.

Abraham and Abimelech – The familiar story of Abraham and Abimelech is found in Genesis 20. By way of quick review, Abraham attempted to pass off his wife, Sarah, as his sister out of fear for his own well-being. God comes to Abimelech in a dream and gives him the truth. Though Abraham lied, God nevertheless has Abraham intercede for the restoration of Abimelech's afflicted household. Do you wonder why? After all, God didn't need Abraham to be the agent of that restoration, but he chose him for that role. Perhaps God desired to teach Abraham by involving him personally in Abimelech's restoration. In any event this is a story that exemplifies how God may ordain someone's intercessory prayer as the means to his decreed end.

Moses Preventing the Destruction of Israel – After the Golden Calf incident, God promised destruction upon Israel in Exodus 32:10:

> *Now therefore let me alone, that my wrath may burn hot against them and I may consume them, in order that I may make a great nation of you.*

Then Moses intercedes:

> *But Moses implored the LORD his God and said, "O LORD, why does your wrath burn hot against your people, whom you have brought out of the land of Egypt with great power and with a mighty hand? Why should the Egyptians say, 'With evil intent did he bring them out, to kill them in the mountains and to consume them from the face of the earth"*

> *Turn from your burning anger and relent from this disaster against your people. Remember Abraham, Isaac, and Israel, your servants, to whom you swore by your own self, and said to them, 'I will multiply your offspring as the stars of heaven, and all this land that I have promised I will give to your offspring, and they shall inherit it forever.'" And the LORD relented from the disaster that he had spoken of bringing on his people.* (Exodus 32:10-14)

This passage teaches us much about intercession and about prayer in general. Moses intercedes based upon the promises, attributes and good name of God. This is not "wishful" intercession, but rather intercession with a crystal clear basis. When God "relents," that is, changes his mind, we are seeing another classic example of anthropomorphism, in that the story is told from our human perspective so that we can understand it more easily. From Moses' perspective, as the author of Exodus, God was going one direction and then switched to the opposite direction – what we would call changing your mind. But from God's perspective, the outcome was settled in eternity past when he decreed that Moses' intercession would be the means by which he would not justly destroy Israel. Ultimately this encounter was a growth experience God designed for Moses as he called him to the role of an intercessor. I daresay that God may call us into challenging situations in order to make us intercessors as well.

Job's Friends – After the resolution of Job's trials, God command his "friends" to go to Job and offer burnt offerings, essentially putting Job in the role of a priest. Then God directed Job to offer intercessory prayer for their sins of presumption against him. Again we see an intercessor as the chosen means to God's end. But why was an intercessor needed? Strictly speaking, an intercessor was not needed, in that God could have directly forgiven the three men. Yet involving Job in the process did two things: First it provided reconciliation in their relationship with Job, and secondly it provided justice to Job for his being falsely accused by his friends.

Jeremiah – I find it interesting that not only does God call his children to intercede for others, but he also may call them *not* to intercede. Such is the case with Jeremiah:

> *As for you, do not pray for this people, or lift up a cry or prayer for them, and do not intercede with me, for I will not hear you . . . Therefore do not pray for this people, or lift up a cry or prayer on their behalf, for I will not listen when they call to me in the time of their trouble.*
> (Jeremiah 7:16; 11:14)

This rebuke to intercession of course comes in a specific context – that of God's judgment upon Judah that resulted in the Babylonian Captivity. Nevertheless I believe this passage teaches us that our prayers of intercession must align with God's will. Don't intercede without a biblical basis and clear leading from the Holy Spirit.

Ezekiel – In Ezekiel we learn the great value God places on intercession and intercessors:

> *And I sought for a man among them who should build up the wall and stand in the breach before me for the land, that I should not destroy it, but I found none.* (Ezekiel 22:30)

Intercessory prayer is clearly part of God's plan. The question is whether we are willing to "stand in the gap" as he leads.

Saul's Conversion – The familiar story of Saul's conversion in Acts 9 also has a lot to teach us about intercessory prayer. God called Ananias to go to Saul and pray for the restoration of his sight. Why did God "need" Ananias – why not just directly heal Saul? Sometimes a human agent is necessary to facilitate reconciliation. Yes, Saul had been reconciled to Jesus Christ, but what about being reconciled to the Christian community he had been persecuting? That needed a person-to-person encounter. Can you imagine how difficult that was for Ananias? Upon being called to go to Saul, Ananias proceeds to "inform" God about Saul's reputation, only to have God say:

> *Go, for he is a chosen instrument of mine to carry my name before the Gentiles and kings and the children of Israel.* (Acts 9:15)

The moral of the story is that intercession isn't always easy. God may direct you to a difficult time of intercession.

Jesus Intercession for Believers – There is no greater example of intercession than that of our Lord in the High Priestly Prayer of John 17. I have devoted a whole chapter to this later.

INTERCESSION FOR CIVIL AUTHORITIES

God calls believers to intercede for civil authorities who, more often than not, are probably unbelievers. The primary passage covering this is I Timothy 2:1-4:

> *First of all, then I urge that supplications, prayers, intercessions, and thanksgivings be made for all people, for kings and all who are in high positions, that we may lead a peaceful and quiet life, godly and dignified in every way. This is good, and it is pleasing in the sight of God our Savior, who desires all people to be saved and to come to the knowledge of the truth.*

This passage presents some interesting challenges, and I believe, is often misinterpreted. Someone might take God's desire for "all people" to be saved to teach universalism, namely that every person will be saved. That, of course, is clearly contradicted by numerous scriptures. More commonly this passage is used, out of context, to deny the doctrine of election, for if God "desires" everyone to be saved, how could certain ones have been chosen before the foundation of the world (Ephesians 1:4)? Again, since over 40 passages in the New Testament clearly teach the doctrine of election or predestination of believers, likewise that cannot be the correct interpretation.

Some try to bridge this gap by suggesting that God, in his heart, may have compassion and "desire" that all would be saved, even though his eternal decree is otherwise. Somehow to me that seems like an attempt to make God schizophrenic, and I definitely don't want to go there! Instead I think the context shows us that the "all people" are those he describes in the verse – "kings and all who are in high positions." In other words, Paul is saying to the church, which is at that time being persecuted by the government, that "all sorts of people" will be saved, even some civil authorities.

However, the emphasis of the intercession prescribed is really more for the benefit of the church "that we may lead a peaceful and quiet life, godly and dignified in every way." God maintains an orderly society in part through the civil government and its laws as taught in Romans 13. An orderly society benefits Christians and makes the work of the church easier. Civil authorities can be an obstacle or a help in the church fulfilling its mission. We intercede for them that they might not hinder the work or people of God.

INTERCESSION FOR SALVATION OF NON-CHRISTIANS

A significant part of the average Christian's intercessory prayers are for the salvation of non-Christians. But is that biblical? Is that a legitimate intercessory petition, or is it "wishing" instead of "praying?"

There is really no example in scripture of praying for an individual to come to Christ. Actually Jesus himself states the *opposite* view in John 17:9:

> *I am praying for them* [the disciples]. *I am not praying for the world but for those whom you have given me, for they are yours.*

That word from the Lord alone should sober us. Jesus' expression here is certainly consistent with the doctrine of election. If someone's ultimate spiritual destiny was decided "before the foundation of the world" (Ephesians 1:4), they are either elect or they're not, and you're intercession isn't going to change God's mind in the matter.

However, your prayers *may* be God's chosen means to bring about his end for that person indeed coming to faith. God has decreed that part of his story, if not most of his story, would be fulfilled through human actions. Be intimate with God and sensitive to his leading. Then intercede for someone's salvation if you are so led, but banish any attitude that the power of your prayers is somehow influencing God to do something he had not already decreed to happen.

Make no mistake for there is much we can legitimately pray for regarding people coming to Christ. Pray *about* people God lays on your heart: "God, what is your plan for this person? How would you use me in their life?" According to scripture it is appropriate to pray that God would convict concerning "sin, righteousness and judgment" (John 16:8-10). Pray for opportunities to witness, given we are called to do that regardless of whether the person responds or not – sow the seed:

> *Finally, brothers, pray for us, that the word of the Lord may speed ahead and be honored, as happened among you* . . . (II Thessalonians 3:1)

Further, pray for the proclamation of the gospel to be clear:

> *. . . and also for me, that words may be given to me in opening my mouth boldly to proclaim the mystery of the gospel.* (Ephesians 6:19)

> *At the same time, pray also for us, that God may open to us a door for the word, to declare the mystery of Christ, on account of which I am in prison* . . . (Colossians 4:3)

Jesus exhorts us to:

> *Then he said to his disciples, "The harvest is plentiful, but the laborers are few; therefore pray earnestly to the Lord of the harvest to send out laborers into his harvest.* (Matthew 9:37-38)

Thus, so much can be *legitimately* prayed regarding reaching people for Christ. Our intercessory prayers are part of God's decreed will for people coming to Christ. Just don't presumptively pray for a specific individual to come to faith unless clearly led to do so.

CONCLUSION

Intercession is indeed a major part of prayer, but it is often done poorly and without biblical basis. The point is to avoid telling God what he must do – that's way above our pay grade! Rather, listen to God and be a part of what he is doing in that person or place.

APPLICATION & IMPLEMENTATION

1. As you receive requests this week for intercessory prayer, first study the Scripture to see if there is a basis before committing to prayer.

2. If you are unsure of a biblical basis for a particular intercessory prayer, ask God to show you what and how you should pray, rather than being presumptive in your intercession.

THIS CHAPTER IN A NUTSHELL

1. Intercessory prayer requires a biblical basis.

2. Intercession is not changing God's mind, but participating in his decreed plan.

3. God involves his children in intercession to bless them, to develop intimacy with them and to bring relational healing to others.

4. Intercession for civil authorities is ultimately for the benefit of God's people and work.

5. Though there is no biblical example of praying for an individual to come to faith in Christ, God may direct and use you as the means to that end.

Chapter 10

Radical Psalms

The more deeply we grow into the Psalms and the more often we pray them as our own, the more simple and rich will our prayer become. — Dietrich Bonhoeffer

When my guts are turned inside out with an agonizing problem, there's always one place I turn to in scripture – the Book of Psalms. Yet, more than anything else in this book, writing about the Psalms is a daunting task. I think of Spurgeon's multi-volume classic commentary, *The Treasury of David*, which I spent a couple years going through in my quiet time, and then ask, "What could I possibly say about the Psalms?" But this chapter is not a commentary on the Psalms, but rather I will use the Psalms to illustrate principles of prayer.

The Psalms are the prayer book of the Bible. These 150 prayers teach us more about prayer than anything I know of. While the Bible is God's Word to us, the Psalms uniquely give us words to express to God. They teach how to talk to God in prayer. In the Psalms we find the entire range of human emotion. Church Father Athanasius (296-373) said of them:

> *I believe that a man can find nothing more glorious than these Psalms; for they embrace the whole life of man, the affection of his mind, and the motions of his soul. To praise and glorify God, he can select a psalm suited to every occasion, and thus will find that they were written for him.*[1]

John Calvin described them as:

> *An anatomy of all parts of the soul.*[2]

If you have a problem, the Psalms address it. If you would learn prayer, the Psalms will teach you the way.

HONEST PRAYER

Perhaps the most striking feature of the Psalms is their brute honesty. There's no posing or pretending here as these men of God spilled their guts before the throne:

- **About Enemies**

  O LORD, how many are my foes! Many are rising against me; many are saying of my soul, there is no salvation for him in God. (3:1-2)

- **About God's Seeming Absence**

  Why, O LORD, do you stand afar off? Why do you hide yourself in times of trouble? (10:1)

  How long, O LORD? Will you forget me forever? How long will you hide your face from me? (13:1)

  My God, my God, why have you forsaken me? Why are you so far from saving me, from the words of my groaning? O my God, I cry by day, but you do not answer, and by night, but I find no rest. (22:1-2)

  O God, why do you cast us off forever? Why does your anger smoke against the sheep of your pasture? (74:1)

  Will the Lord spurn forever and never again be favorable? Has his steadfast love forever ceased? Are his promises at an end for all time? Has God forgotten to be gracious? Has he in anger shut up his compassion? (77:7-9)

They really let it all hang out without pretense. Yet this is not a faithless murmuring or doubting, but rather a submissive worshipful complaint. It is honest complaint, but without casting blame upon God. Interestingly though, while many psalms *start* with complaint, they end in faithful assurance of God's providence, as in Psalm 13:

> *But I have trusted in your steadfast love; my heart shall rejoice in your salvation. I will sing to the LORD, because he has dealt bountifully*

> *with me.* (13:5-6)

PSALMS HIGHLIGHT PRAISE

We best learn what it means to praise God in the Psalms. Some begin with praise while many end with praise in showing us how to relate to our awesome God. In Psalm 3, after beginning with complaint, David turns to praise:

> *But you, O LORD, are a shield about me, my glory, and the lifter of my head.* (3:3)

A similar pattern is noted in Psalm 5:

> *O LORD, in the morning you hear my voice; in the morning I prepare a sacrifice for you and watch. For you are not a God who delights in wickedness; evil may not dwell with you.* (5:3-4)

Note that praise, as discussed in our earlier chapter, is characterized by "You are . . ." statements.

Psalm 8 is a classic of praise as David gazes into the night sky:

> *O LORD, our Lord, how majestic is your name in all the earth! You have set your glory above the heavens. Out of the mouth of babes and infants, you have established strength because of your foes, to still the enemy and the avenger. When I look at your heavens, the work of your fingers, the moon and the stars, which you have set in place, what is man that you are mindful of him, and the son of man that you care for him?* (8:1-4)

Psalm 18 would teach us how to express love to God as praise:

> *I love you, O LORD, my strength. The LORD is my rock and my fortress and my deliverer, my God, my rock, in whom I take refuge, my shield, and the horn of my salvation, my stronghold. I call upon the LORD, who is worthy to be praised, and I am saved from my enemies.* (18:1-3)

David contemplation turns to rapture as he simply runs out of words to describe his delight in God. Oh that we might catch that same passion! This long psalm continues heaping praise after praise. You will find praise throughout the Psalms. The question we must ask is, "Is praise found throughout my prayers?"

PSALMS OF THANKSGIVING

Thanksgiving in prayer is really quite common and requires little instruction. Though thanksgiving can lead to praise, we often just stop at thanksgiving without moving on to praise when we pray. Unlike many of our prayers, many prayers in the Psalms start with thanksgiving, but then move quickly to praise as the greater expression, as in Psalm 118:

> *Oh give thanks to the LORD, for he is good; for his steadfast love endures forever! Let Israel say, "His steadfast love endures forever." Let the house of Aaron say, "His steadfast love endures forever." Let those who fear the LORD say, "his steadfast love endures forever." Out of my distress I called on the LORD; the LORD answered me and set me free. The LORD is on my side, I will not fear. What can man do to me?* (118:1-6)

The psalm then continues between statements of thanksgiving (what God has done) and praise (who God is).

Psalm 136 is perhaps the most familiar psalm of thanksgiving with its antiphonal liturgy in all 26 verses repeating the phrase:

> *Give thanks to the LORD, for he is good, for his steadfast love endures forever.*

Recounting God's marvelous work from the Creation through the Wilderness Wandering, this repetition demonstrates the profound importance of remembering and thanking God for what he has done for us. The key concept, however, is to not stop at thanksgiving, but rather to let it usher you into praise of God.

PSALMS OF PROTECTION AND DELIVERANCE

Much of particularly David's prayers in the Psalms request protection and deliverance from enemies – of which he had many! That was David's life as a warrior king, but what about us today? We individually or corporately as the Church, have enemies as well as we walk in the midst of a rebellious human race. Frankly, if you don't have any enemies, you're probably not doing anything that significantly challenges the kingdom of darkness.

Let's look at some of the many examples of such prayers in the Psalms. Going back to Psalm 3 we read:

> *Arise, O LORD! Save me, O my God! For you strike all my enemies on the cheek; you break the teeth of the wicked.* (3:7)

In Psalm 5 he prays for deliverance, not merely for his own preservation, but as God's man:

> *Lead me, O LORD, in your righteousness because of my enemies; make your way straight before me.* (5:8)

One of the richest psalms, and probably my personal favorite, is Psalm 34, which deals with deliverance and much more:

> *I sought the LORD, and he answered me and delivered me from all my fears. Those who look to him are radiant, and their faces shall never be ashamed. This poor man cried, and the LORD heard him and saved him out of all his troubles. The angel of the LORD encamps around those who fear him, and delivers them.* (34:4-7)

This psalm reflects strong passion borne of an intimate relationship with God. Perhaps the most familiar psalm of deliverance and protection is Psalm 91, previously referred to in the "Petition" chapter:

> *He who dwells in the shelter of the Most High will abide in the shadow of the Almighty. I will say to the LORD, "My refuge and my fortress, my God, in whom I trust." For he will deliver you from the snare of the fowler and from the deadly pestilence. He will cover you with his pinions, and under his wings you will find refuge; his faithfulness is a shield and*

buckler. You will not fear the terror of the night nor the arrow that flies by day, nor the pestilence that stalks in darkness, nor the destruction that wastes at noonday. (91:1-6)

The entire psalm goes into much more detail on the promised deliverance. Note again the relational context as the author first describes the one to whom this promise applies – "He who dwells in the shelter of the Most High." If God is protecting you for his purposes, nothing will touch you, but don't be presumptive. One of my professors related praying this prayer for his brother as he went off to World War II only to realize his error of presumption in later years. God often chooses to be glorified through the sickness and death of his children. Our focus must remain on the fact that God's will be done, and that nothing adverse will happen outside of that will.

PSALMS OF GUIDANCE

One of the most frequent prayers – both in the Psalms and for us – concerns guidance. To tell the truth, studying this topic of prayer in the Psalms was an eye-opener for me. Usually when you or I pray for guidance, we are praying for what to do in some given situation:

What job to take

What school to go to

What person to marry

What purchase to make

How to do some task confronting us

Interestingly, there's really none of that in the Psalms concerning guidance. The guidance or direction in the Psalms has a rather singular focus:

Lead me into faithfully following God

That's what we read in Psalm 5:

> *Lead me, O LORD, in your righteousness because of my enemies; make your way straight before me.* (5:8)

What is the "way" that he wants to be made straight before him? Is it about his daily life choices? Hardly, since he prays to be led in God's "righteousness." David's prayer is that his way would be aligned with God's way to the end that he would not be a reproach before his enemies. This is even clearer in Psalm 31:

> *For you are my rock and my fortress; and for your name's sake you lead me and guide me.* (31:3)

David's wish isn't to know which pair of sandals to buy, but that God's name would not be disparaged. His focus is constantly on God's glorification rather than the fulfillment of his personal needs. Also note in this passage that he doesn't really *ask* for guidance, but rather *presumes* it in a statement of praise. Because of his relationship with God, he praises God and presumes he will be led by God.

Psalm 32:8 is a favorite that I have probably taken out of context more times than I can count:

> *I will instruct you and teach you in the way you should go; I will counsel you with my eye upon you.*

Have you ever claimed that promise for some decision you needed to make? But is that what it's really about? Again the context points to being guided in the ways of God – being kept on his narrow path. Thus I can't legitimately use that promise praying about some business decision – should I do choice A or choice B. But I can pray confidently that God would direct me in his way, his word and his commandments.

Let's look at Psalm 48:12-14 for another insight on guidance:

> *Walk about Zion, go around her, number her towers, consider well her ramparts, go through her citadels, that you may tell the next generation that this is God, our God forever and ever. He will guide us forever.*

The psalmist looks at what God has done in providing the fortress of Zion as a provision for his people. From God's past performance he deduces that there will be future guidance as well. As in the previous examples, this "guidance" centers on the fulfillment of God's purposes rather than daily "Should I do this or that?" decisions.

Psalm 73 emphasizes the relational aspect of God's guidance:

> *Nevertheless, I am continually with you; you hold my right hand. You guide me with your counsel, and afterward you will receive me to glory.* (73:23-24)

While you and I typically just ask God to guide us on some particular decision, Asaph sought guidance as an outgrowth of his relationship with God. In his mind everything centers on God and the fulfillment of his purposes, not on the psalmists perceived needs.

Let me offer a couple more examples of prayers for guidance in the Psalms. Psalm 119:35 makes a simple prayer petition that shows us the right way to seek guidance:

> *Lead me in the path of your commandments, for I delight in it.*

Though God can and does lead us in everyday decisions, the emphasis here again is clearly on being led in a path of obedience to God. The psalmist recognizes how very difficult it is to follow God's ways fully apart from divine intervention. It is as if his life is laser focused to maintaining an alignment with the ways of the Lord. Note his "delight" in that prospect. This is not a man who *uses* God to fulfill his desires, but rather a man who wants to fulfill God's desires.

How permanent and sure is God's guidance of his children? Psalm 139 tells us:

> *If I take the wings of the morning and dwell in the uttermost parts of the sea, even there your hand shall lead me, and your right hand shall hold me.* (139:9-10)

What a description of a relationship with one who is perfectly faithful and trustworthy! God's care in both "holding" and "leading" him knows no bounds of space or time.

A final passage of a prayer for guidance in Psalm 143 serves as a great summary:

> *Let me hear in the morning of your steadfast love, for in you I trust. Make me know the way I should go, for to you I lift up my soul. Deliver me from my enemies, O LORD! I have fled to you for refuge! Teach me to do your will, for you are my God! Let your good Spirit lead me on level ground!* (143:8-10)

From beginning to end this prayer for guidance is relational. It begins with an acknowledgement of God's love which generates the psalmist's trust. He desires direction in that relationship with God, to the end that he might do his will.

PSALMS OF PROVISION

Perhaps more than any other prayer, we pray for provision of basic needs. This common petition is found in the Psalms as well as throughout the Bible. The Lord's Prayer might first come to mind with its petition, "Give us this day our daily bread." We'll cover the Lord's Prayer in later chapter, but for now let's start with Psalm 23:

> *The LORD is my shepherd; I shall not want. He makes me lie down in green pastures. He leads me beside still waters. He restores my soul. He leads me in paths of righteousness for his name's sake. Even though I walk through the valley of the shadow of death, I will fear no evil, for you are with me; your rod and your staff, they comfort me. You prepare a table before me in the presence of my enemies; you anoint my head with oil; my cup overflows. Surely goodness and mercy shall follow me all the days of my life, and I shall dwell in the house of the LORD forever.*

What a simple and perfect prayer! Various books detail the parallels the psalm presents between the shepherd's care for his sheep and our needs. Jesus explained this further in John 10 in describing himself as "the good shepherd."

Does it strike you that, though this is a "psalm of provision," David doesn't ask for anything? That surely isn't the way we typically pray for provision. Instead of *asking* God to provide, David simply says that God *is* providing. The psalm is a prayerful confession of who God is and what he is like. It is a psalm of praise. Because he knows the character of God and God's past provisions, he simply trusts present and future provision. He petitions in complete faith, assured of an affirmative answer.

Let's again turn to Psalm 34 for another example:

> *Oh, fear the LORD, you his saints, for those who fear him have no lack! The young lions suffer want and hunger; but those who seek the LORD lack no good thing.* (34:9-10)

As we see repeatedly in the Psalms, God's provision is in a relational context. Within this relationship basic needs are met and no "good" thing is lacking. Often to our dismay, what we would *think* is a "good" thing, is not judged good by God and is therefore not provided. His definition of "good," based on his eternal plans and purposes will always prevail. Psalm 84 is another favorite of provision with its final verse:

> *For the LORD God is a sun and shield; the LORD bestows favor and honor. No good thing does he withhold from those who walk uprightly.* (84:11)

Like Psalm 23 and 34 we have a statement of praise to God for who he is. Rather than petition God for provision, the psalmist simply states that God will appropriately provide. Now think about that a moment: Isn't that really superior to having to ask? Do your kids have to ask for every provision, or do they know, based upon your character and past provision, that you will provide? Perhaps this concept is best summarized by Jesus in the Sermon on the Mount as noted earlier:

> *Therefore do not be anxious, saying, "What shall we eat?" or "What shall we drink?" or "What shall we wear?" For the Gentiles seek after*

all these things, and your heavenly Father knows that you need them all. But seek first the kingdom of God and his righteousness, and all these things will be added to you. (Matthew 6:31-33)

PSALMS OF JUSTICE

Many psalms cry out for justice for God's people. They are known as the **imprecatory psalms** -- imprecate meaning to pray evil against someone. These psalms call down divine justice on the wicked and cursing on the enemies of God. The list of imprecatory psalms includes 5, 10, 17, 35, 58, 59, 69, 70, 79, 83, 109, 129, 137 and 140. Interpreting the imprecatory psalms is challenging and controversial, to say the least. Frankly, this is territory neither for the weak of stomach nor the faint of heart. Let me give a couple of examples:

Contend, O LORD, with those who contend with me; fight against those who fight against me! . . . Let them be put to shame and dishonor who seek after my life! Let them be turned back and disappointed who devise evil against me! Let them be like chaff before the wind, with the angel of the LORD driving them away! Let their way be dark and slippery, with the angel of the LORD pursuing them! (35:1, 4-6)

Let their own table before them become a snare; and when they are at peace, let it become a trap. Let their eyes be darkened, so that they cannot see, and make their loins tremble continually. Pour out your indignation upon them, and let your burning anger overtake them. May their camp be a desolation; let no one dwell in their tents. For they persecute him whom you have struck down, and they recount the pain of those you have wounded. Add to them punishment upon punishment; may they have no acquittal from you. Let them be blotted out of the book of the living; let them not be enrolled among the righteous. (69:22-28)

Regrettably, the typical contemporary Christian interpretation of these psalms can be summed up in one word – **denial.** There is generally some attempt to water these down, simply because they don't sound very nice to most Christians today. Some typical interpretations include:

- Israel was uniquely called to be an instrument of God's justice, but we are now in the New Covenant as a dispensation of grace.
- The Old Testament presents a "sub-Christian" ethic that enlightened believers no longer believe. This view would be typically found with apostate, liberal theologians who do not accept the authority of scripture in the first place.
- Christ bore God's judgment for sin and thus gave a new commandment to love your enemies instead of cursing them.
- God's people now engage in a spiritual "war" against satanic forces rather than the Old Testament wars against godless nations.
- Some would write off these psalms as expressions of what the psalmists were *feeling* at moments of rage, but for which they had no divine approval.

The idea of minimizing or "weaseling out" of the plain sense of the imprecatory psalms has never sat well with me, first because of II Timothy 3:16-17:

> *All Scripture* [speaking here of the Old Testament] *is breathed out by God and profitable for teaching, for reproof, for correction, and for training in righteousness, that the man of God may be competent, equipped for every good work.*

That is a very big hurdle to jump for the Christian who would deny the relevance of any part of the Bible.

One of the most helpful insights I ever received on this came from a pastor who noted that one's acceptance of the contemporary validity of the imprecatory psalms depends largely on how much you've been abused by godless people. If you've never been attacked with a frivolous lawsuit, persecuted by a government agency, maligned in the media with distorted reporting, robbed by employees or betrayed by people you trusted, you will probably wince at the Psalms of judgment. But if your story is all of the above (as is mine) you will find these psalms not only appropriate, but comforting.

Let me take issue particularly with the view that Christ bore the judgment for sin, and thus it is no longer appropriate for Christians to call down God's judgment on anyone. The often debated Reformation doctrine of *particular atonement* comes into play here, which essentially says Christ paid for the sin of his chosen children, i.e. "the elect," not for the sins of every person in the world. His death was *sufficient* to save everyone, but only *efficient* to save those chosen from before the foundation of the world (Ephesians 1:4). Thus, the unbeliever's sin is not covered by Christ – otherwise no one could justly be sent to hell. How could a just God allow someone whose sin was paid for to pay it a second time in hell?

Yet there remains a greater point: imprecations are also found in the New Testament. You can't make this an Old Covenant issue when we find these New Testament examples:

> *But whenever you enter a town and they do not receive you, go into its streets and say, "Even the dust of your town that clings to our feet we wipe off against you. Nevertheless know this, that the kingdom of God has come near."* (Lk 10:10-11)

> *But even if we or an angel from heaven should preach to you a gospel contrary to the one we preached to you, let him be accursed.* (Gal. 1:8)

> *If anyone has no love for the Lord, let him be accursed. Our LORD, come!* (I Cor. 16:22)

The real clincher, however, concerns Peter citing an imprecation from Psalm 69:25 relative to the betrayal of Judas:

> *For it is written in the Book of Psalms, "May his camp become desolate, and let there be no one to dwell in it."* (Acts 1:20)

He then cites a second imprecation, this time from Psalm 109:8:

> *Let another take his office.*

If imprecation is just Old Testament stuff, why do we find it in the New Testament as well? Could it be that it's because the same God "breathed out" both Old and New Testament?

Now that I've made a case for the justice psalms, let me put on the brakes a bit. This is not license to go out and start cursing everyone who's ever crossed you in some way. The imprecatory psalms, correctly used, do not express personal vengeance, but rather call on divine justice. We don't curse our enemies; God does (Romans 12:14, 19). Writing on this, Jason Jackson notes:

> *David is not praying to God out of malice and vindictiveness against someone he dislikes personally. It is not a matter of personal revenge; rather, these "harsh" statements reflect David's awareness of God's justice and his intolerance for sin.*[3]

Dr. Walter Kaiser, whom I was privileged to have as an Old Testament professor decades ago wrote:

> *They [these hard sayings] are not statements of personal vendetta, but they are utterances of zeal for the kingdom of God and his glory. To be sure, the attacks which provoked these prayers were not from personal enemies; rather, they were rightfully seen as attacks against God and especially his representatives in the promised line of the Messiah.*[4]

In the final analysis our motivation with any usage of these psalms of justice must be zeal for God's Kingdom and for his will to prevail. Imprecation should apply *only* to those who refuse to repent.

PRAYING THE PSALMS

After discussing the various types of prayer in the Psalms, what's the how-to? How can you begin to implement using the Bible's prayer book in your own life? Let me suggest a few steps:

- Find a psalm that fits your current situation and expresses your felt emotion.
- Pray that psalm back to God, changing the words where required.
- Take time for silence – listening – as part of this prayer.
- Pause to meditate on the most meaningful parts.
- Focus not on petitioning God so much as just spending time in his presence, developing your relationship with him.

The Book of Psalms is God's great gift to teach us prayer. Next, let's look at three Bible characters who exemplify what our prayers should look like.

APPLICATION & IMPLEMENTATION

1. Choose a psalm that mirrors your greatest current need and pray it. Observe how that affects your prayer life.

2. Consider making reading and praying the Psalms part of your daily quiet time. For example, reading five per day requires one month to complete the Book of Psalms.

THIS CHAPTER IN A NUTSHELL

1. The Psalms teach us how to speak to God in prayer.

2. The Psalms show that it's okay to lay honest complaint before God.

3. The best instruction in how to praise God is found in the Psalms.

4. Petition in the Psalms focuses on being led into faithfully following God and his ways.

5. The imprecatory psalms do not call for personal vengeance, but rather for divine justice.

FOOTNOTES:

1. Calvin, John, Commentary on the book of Psalms, (Grand Rapids: Baker, 1979), Vol 1, xxxvi-xxxvii.

2. Bushell, Michael, The Songs of Zion, (Pittsburgh: Crown and Covenant, 1980), 94.

3. Jackson, Jason. "Do the Imprecatory Psalms and Christian Ethics Clash? ChristianCourier.com. https://www.christiancourier.com/articles/1156-do-the-imprecatory-psalms-and-christian-ethics-clash)

4. Kaiser, Walter, *Hard Sayings of the Old Testament*, (Downers Grove, IL: InterVarsity Press), 1988 p. 172.

Chapter 11

Radical Examples – Hannah, Daniel & Paul

Conversation with God leads to an encounter with God.[1] — Tim Keller

Is there a greater teaching method than a good example? I doubt it, though sometimes a good example can be convicting. Seeing the vast difference between prayers in the Bible and my own prayers motivated me to write this book, as I recognized how pathetic my prayers were by comparison. While there are many notable examples of prayer in the Bible, I've chosen three characters to highlight – Hannah, Daniel and Paul.

HANNAH'S FIRST PRAYER

The brief story of Hannah is found in the first two chapters of I Samuel. To review the story, Hannah was one of two wives of Elkanah. Though greatly loved by her husband, Hannah was barren – the ultimate curse for a woman during that time and culture. She desperately wanted a son, little knowing how significant that son would be in God's overall plan.

We actually have two prayers of Hannah recorded, the first of which is her petition, while the second is praise for the answer to her prayer. She goes to the Tabernacle to pray, this of course being before the temple was built. She is devastated and desperate, weeping bitterly as she prays:

> *O LORD of hosts, if you will indeed look on the affliction of your servant and remember me and not forget your servant, but will give to your servant a son, then I will give him to the LORD all the days of his life, and no razor shall touch his head.* (I Samuel 1:11)

What do we see in her prayer? Like the psalmists, she begins with honest complaint, letting it all hang out, being fully transparent with

God as to her distress. Yet even in her complaint, she begins by praising God with the simple phrase, "O LORD of hosts." No doubt exists here as to her submission to God.

Hannah's petition is a vow, and I wonder why? She could have asked for a son without making a vow. Was this the Spirit's leading to her in this situation? Perhaps, but possibly she was so very desperate that she believed the only way God would give her a son (and remove the reproach of barrenness) was if she would sacrifice that son back to God for his service. It was biblical for her to make a vow, though the Mosaic Law did state that a rash vow could be nullified by her husband (Numbers 30:6-15). By way of application to us today, we should at the very least be careful with making vows. Vows are serious, as noted in Ecclesiastes 5:4-6:

> *When you vow a vow to God, do not delay paying it, for he has no pleasure in fools. Pay what you vow. It is better that you should not vow than that you should vow and not pay.*

Likewise vows were not prohibited by Jesus in the Sermon on the Mount (Matthew 5:33-37), though he did condemn improper, deceitful oaths.

The spiritual obtuse priest Eli sees her lips moving without audible sound and jumps to the false conclusion that she is drunk. His rebuke, of course, would have been considerably more applicable to his own wicked sons rather than the godly Hannah. Nevertheless, Eli is the priest and thus represents men to God. He grants her petition in the name of God, not knowing what exactly she was praying for. At Eli's pronouncement Hannah believes and leaves with assurance:

> *Then the woman went her way and ate, and her face was no longer sad.*
> (I Samuel 1:18b)

HANNAH'S SECOND PRAYER

Hannah becomes pregnant and gives birth to Samuel. She remains at home with him until he is weaned – probably around age three. Then, in fulfillment of her vow, she returns to the Tabernacle to worship, offer sacrifice and present Samuel to Eli. Imagine the emotion involved in a mother giving up her three year-old son. While Hannah could understandably weep, instead she worships God as we read in her second prayer. Not only is this a prayer of exalted praise, but it is also prophetic in looking toward what God will do through Samuel:

> *My heart exults in the LORD; my strength is exalted in the LORD. My mouth derides my enemies, because I rejoice in your salvation. There is none holy like the LORD; there is none besides you; there is no rock like our God. Talk no more so very proudly, let not arrogance come from your mouth; for the LORD is a God of knowledge, and by him actions are weighed. The bows of the mighty are broken, but the feeble bind on strength. Those who were full have hired themselves out for bread, but those who were hungry have ceased to hunger. The barren has borne seven, but she who has many children is forlorn. The LORD kills and brings to life; he brings down to Sheol and raises up. The LORD makes poor and makes rich; he brings low and he exalts. He raises up the poor from the dust; he lifts the needy from the ash heap to make them sit with princes and inherit a seat of honor. For the pillars of the earth are the LORD's, and on them he has set the world. He will guard the feet of his faithful ones, but the wicked shall be cut off in darkness, for not by might shall a man prevail. The adversaries of the LORD shall be broken to pieces; against them he will thunder in heaven. The LORD will judge the ends of the earth; he will give strength to his king and exalt the power of his anointed.* (I Samuel 2:1-10)

What stands out to you in this prayer? What do we learn? First of all, it is a classic example of praise. Praise doesn't get any better than this! Secondly, note there is no petition in this prayer at all as she praises God's holiness, knowledge, judgment, provision, sovereignty, goodness, mercy and protection. Her thanksgiving to God for providing Samuel in response to her petition moves her to praise. When was the last time you prayed like this, or have you ever prayed like this? This woman has experienced God's miraculous intervention in her life. Her relationship with God is in a state of rapture. If we want to learn how to praise God, we need look no further than Hannah.

DANIEL'S PRAYER FOR HIS PEOPLE

Speaking of prayers that look nothing like the way most of us pray, let's turn to Daniel for another example. This extensive prayer for his people in the Babylonian Captivity features praise, confession and petition:

> *In the first year of Darius the son of Ahasuerus, by descent a Mede, who was made king over the realm of the Chaldeans – in the first year of his reign, I, Daniel, perceived in the books the number of years that, according to the word of the LORD to Jeremiah the prophet, must pass before the end of the desolations of Jerusalem, namely, seventy years.*
>
> *Then I turned my face to the Lord God, seeking him by prayer and pleas for mercy with fasting and sackcloth and ashes. I prayed to the LORD my God and made confession, saying, O Lord, the great and awesome God, who keeps covenant and steadfast love with those who love him and keep his commandment, we have sinned and done wrong and acted wickedly and rebelled, turning aside from your commandments and rules. We have not listened to your servants the prophets, who spoke in your name to our kings, our princes, and our father, and to all the people of the land, To you, O Lord, belongs righteousness, but to us open shame, as at this day, to the men of Judah, to the inhabitants of Jerusalem, and to all Israel, those who are near and those who are far away, in all the lands to which you have driven them, because of the treachery that they have committed against you. To us, O LORD, belongs open shame, to our kings, to our princes, and to our fathers, because we have sinned against you.*
>
> *To the Lord our God belong mercy and forgiveness, for we have rebelled against him and have not obeyed the voice of the LORD our God by walking in his laws, which he set before us by his servants the prophets. All Israel has transgressed your law and turned aside, refusing to obey your voice. And the curse and oath that are written in the Law of Moses the servant of God have been poured out upon us, because we have sinned against him. He has confirmed his words, which he spoke against us and against our rulers who ruled us, by bringing upon us a great calamity. For under the whole heaven there has not been done anything like what has been done against Jerusalem. As it is written in the Law of Moses,*

> *all this calamity has come upon us; yet we have not entreated the favor of the LORD our God, turning from our iniquities and gaining insight by your truth.*
>
> *Therefore the LORD has kept ready the calamity and has brought it upon us, for the LORD our God is righteous in all the works that he has done, and we have not obeyed his voice. And now, O Lord our God, who brought your people out of the land of Egypt with a mighty hand, and have made a name for yourself, as at this day, we have sinned, we have done wickedly. "O Lord, according to all your righteous acts, let your anger and your wrath turn away from your city Jerusalem, your holy hill, because for our sins, and for the iniquities of our fathers, Jerusalem and your people have become a byword among all who are around us.*
>
> *Now therefore, O our God, listen to the prayer of your servant and to his pleas for mercy, and for your own sake, O Lord, make your face to shine upon your sanctuary, which is desolate. O my God, incline your ear and hear. Open your eyes and see our desolations, and the city that is called by your name. For we do not present our pleas before you because of our righteousness, but because of your great mercy. O Lord, hear; O Lord, forgive. O Lord, pay attention and act. Delay not, for your own sake, O my God, because your city and your people are called by your name."*
> (Daniel 9:1-19)

It's not hard to see, looking at this prayer, why Daniel was called "beloved of God." This is what real, mature prayer looks like. We find Daniel's motivation for this prayer in verse 2:

> *. . . in the first year of his reign, I Daniel, perceived in the books the number of years that, according to the word of the LORD to Jeremiah the prophet, must pass before the end of the desolations of Jerusalem, namely, seventy years.*

Daniel read the Bible and knew the prophecy of Jeremiah 25:12 regarding the seventy year captivity in Babylon. He had a **basis** for his prayer. He wasn't just "wishing" for the captivity in Babylon to be over out of personal desire. Instead he brings a petition to God aligned with what God has said. O that we would apply this simple principle! Have a basis for your prayers of petition.

His prayer begins with a confession of sin – an itemized confession of sin:

- We have sinned (v. 5)
- We have not listened to the prophets (v. 6)
- To us belong open shame (v. 8)
- We have rebelled against God (v. 9)
- We have not obeyed the voice of the Lord (v. 10)
- We have sinned against him (v. 11)
- We have not entreated the favor of the Lord (v. 13)
- We have done wickedly (v. 15)

Let's not forget who is uttering these confessions of sin – It is Daniel, of all people – Daniel, identified in the Bible as one of the three most righteous men:

> *Son of man, when a land sins against me by acting faithlessly, and I stretch out my hand against it and break its supply of bread and send famine upon it, and cut off from it man and beast, even if these three men, Noah, Daniel, and Job, were in it, they would deliver but their own lives by their righteousness, declares the Lord GOD.* (Ezekiel 14:13-14)

Though we would be hard pressed to link any sin in Daniel to the Babylonian Captivity, he still identifies with his nation's sin. We stand before God as individuals, but we also are part of nations that have corporately sinned against God. If one of the most righteous men ever had to begin his prayer with confession of sin, how could we not do the same, recognizing our utter inability to come into the presence of God apart from the covering of Christ?

Recognizing the gravity of his own concerns, Daniel also prepares himself to seek God. He humbles himself with fasting (Psalm 69:10) and began with pleas for mercy. Ironically the one who could be considered the most righteous man has the keenest awareness of his own depravity. There is no self-righteousness on display here.

Not surprisingly, Daniel's prayer begins with praise. Confession is necessitated by the acknowledgment of who God is. When we praise the majestic attributes of God, our own inherent sinfulness becomes manifest, demanding our confession of sin. Daniel contrasts the perfections of God with the failings of man with "to you" and "to us" statements:

>To You – Righteousness, mercy and forgiveness
>To Us – Open shame and calamity

With Daniel there is no equivocation on the sinfulness of mankind. In language reminiscent of Romans 3, he states:

> *. . . we have sinned and done wrong and acted wickedly and rebelled, turning aside from your commandments and rules.* (9:5)

It is also noteworthy that he did not try to shift the blame to bad leaders of the nation:

> *He has confirmed his words, which he spoke against us and against our rulers who ruled us, by bringing upon us a great calamity.* (9:12a)

He emphasizes "Against us *and* against our rulers." Daniel fully embraces responsibility for the sin of his nation.

After this lengthy confession, he proceeds to his actual petitions. There are twelve verses of confession, but only three of petition – probably a good ratio for all of us. He petitions:

- Hear our prayers for mercy (v. 17)
- Bless your sanctuary (v. 17)
- Have mercy on our desolations (v. 17-18)

Then in verse 19 he summarizes – hear, forgive, pay attention, act. He concludes his petition providing a "why" God should grant his requests – because of God's name. He asks not for personal benefit or the benefit of his people. He asks not out of any sense of being deserving – quite the contrary. He appeals to God's reputation: In effect, "What will people think of you, O God, if you do not deliver your people from exile as you promised?" In our earlier chapter on order and argument in prayer, Spurgeon emphasized this same point. Be honest – When you petition God, especially for something really big like this was for Daniel, are you concerned with God's reputation or just your own desires? Perhaps after Daniel's extensive confession of sin, only God's reputation and not his desires seemed appropriate.

DANIEL'S ANSWER TO PRAYER

The answer came quickly, delivered by the angel, Gabriel, himself:

> *While I was speaking and praying, confessing my sin and the sin of my people Israel, and presenting my plea before the LORD my God for the holy hill of my God, while I was speaking in prayer, the man Gabriel, whom I had seen in the vision at the first, came to me in swift flight at the time of the evening sacrifice. He made me understand, speaking with me and saying, "O Daniel, I have now come out to give you insight and understanding. At the beginning of your pleas for mercy a word went out, and I have come to tell it to you, for you are greatly loved. Therefore consider the word and understand the vision.* (9:20-23)

Isn't it interesting that God's answer went forth at the beginning of Daniel's pleas for mercy? It seems God has a special place in his heart for his children's cries for mercy, just as in Jesus' parable of the Pharisee and the Tax Collector:

> *"But the tax collector, standing far off, would not even lift up his eyes to heaven, but beat his breast, saying, 'God, be merciful to me, a sinner!' I tell you, this man went down to his house justified, rather than the other. For everyone who exalts himself will be humbled, but the one who humbles himself will be exalted."* (Luke 18:13-14)

Daniel got a lot more than he bargained for in the answer to his prayer. It seems he was only petitioning for a return from exile in accord with the promise given to Jeremiah. Instead, he was given wisdom and understanding (v. 22) because he was greatly loved by God (v. 23). I would parenthetically add that we also are greatly loved, as repeatedly stated by Jesus in the context of answered prayer:

> *If you abide in me, and my words abide in you, ask whatever you wish,*

> *and it will be done for you. By this my Father is glorified, that you bear much fruit and so prove to be my disciples. As the Father has loved me, so have I loved you. Abide in my love.* (John 15:7-9)
>
> *In that day you will ask in my name, and I do not say to you that I will ask the Father on your behalf; for the Father himself loves you, because you have loved me and have believed that I came from God.* (John 16:26-27)

Daniel's answer is the great prophecy of the seventy weeks, laying out the then future coming of the Messiah and the 70 AD destruction of the temple in Jerusalem. Jesus reiterates and amplifies this prophecy in the Olivet Discourse in Matthew 24. Just as Daniel's answer was a bit different than his petition requested, so often will our prayers yield unexpected answers.

PAUL'S PRAYERS FOR BELIEVERS

Paul's epistles reveal his prayers and provide wonderful examples of radical prayer according to the will of God. Our objective is simply to pray biblically, and there is no better way of doing that than following the examples of the prophets, apostles and Jesus Christ himself.

Paul's prayers find their context in his pastoral care for the various Gentile churches. Now you're probably not a pastor of a congregation, but you can pray these same prayers for yourself and your family, plus other believers you are called to intercede for. You can know these petitions are the will of God and thus pray them in faith with utmost confidence. You really can't go wrong with these prayers.

First, let's look at Ephesians 1:15-23:

> *For this reason, because I have heard of your faith in the Lord Jesus and your love toward all the saints, I do not cease to give thanks for you, remembering you in my prayers, that the God of our Lord Jesus Christ, the Father of glory, may give you the Spirit of wisdom and of revelation in the knowledge of him, having the eyes of your hearts enlightened, that you may know what is the hope to which he has called you, what are the*

> *riches of his glorious inheritance in the saints, and what is the immeasurable greatness of his power toward us who believe, according to the working of his great might that he worked in Christ when he raised him from the dead and seated him at his right hand in the heavenly places, far above all rule and authority and power and dominion, and above every name that is named, not only in this age but also in the one to come. And he put all things under his feet and gave him as head over all things to the church, which is his body, the fullness of him who fills all in all.*

The Apostle begins by giving thanks for new believers (v. 15). Why does he give thanks to God? Because God is the one that brought them to a saving knowledge of Christ. If the believers accomplished coming to Christ through their own wisdom, he would thank them for coming to faith, not God. Every Christian can and should give thanks to God for those who come to faith. When you pray this way, be confident you are praying biblically.

Next he prays they would have wisdom and revelation in the knowledge of God (v. 17). What might we infer from this prayer? God wants us to know him better, but we must understand this is a supernatural process – note he prays for a "spirit" of wisdom and revelation. You don't get to know God from fleshly efforts. Like any father, God wants his children to grow and mature. You'll never go wrong in praying for growth in your knowledge of God. What a major need that is for all of us!

Finally, he prays for the "eyes of your heart" to be enlightened, in order that we would know the hope of our calling, our rich spiritual inheritance and the greatness of his resurrection power in us. Why is he praying for heart enlightenment? The goal is not mere intellectual knowledge, but rather heart knowledge felt at the depth of our inner being. Just knowing spiritual truths is empty and futile apart from those truths becoming real at the heart level.

Pray to know the hope of your calling. We need to be reminded in this fallen world that we're called to something so much greater and better. God would have us pray for this sustenance to get us successfully through this life. Pray to experience Christ's resurrection power. We don't have the power to live the Christian life. We absolutely need that power that raised Jesus form the dead to make us alive as well. Praying for these things generates confidence knowing you are petitioning for a request that is most definitely God's will.

Let's turn now to Ephesians 3:14-19:

> *For this reason I bow my knees before the Father, from whom every family in heaven and on earth is named, that according to the riches of his glory he may grant you to be strengthened with power through his Spirit in your inner being, so that Christ may dwell in your hearts through faith—that you, being rooted and grounded in love, may have strength to comprehend with all the saints what is the breadth and length and height and depth, and to know the love of Christ that surpasses knowledge, that you may be filled with all the fullness of God.*

The passage begins with "For this reason," referring to the earlier statements in the chapter concerning the "mystery" of the Gospel – namely that the Gentiles have been grafted into God's family. This isn't just "good" news, but "great" news. We got a pardon from a certain death sentence – and all as an act of grace and mercy from God. In light of this amazing grace, Paul prays for believers to have inner strength, to comprehend the love of Christ and to be spiritually filled. Pray that for yourself in complete confidence that God will grant your petitions.

Looking at Ephesians 4:1-3 we see not a prayer, but a clear statement of the will of God for which we would do well to pray:

> *I therefore, a prisoner for the Lord, urge you to walk in a manner worthy of the calling to which you have been called, with all humility and gentleness, with patience, bearing with one another in love, eager to maintain the unity of the Spirit in the bond of peace.*

We note the "therefore," meaning that based upon all that God has done in bringing us to Christ, we are to respond by walking in a manner worthy of that gift. That "manner worthy" is described as consisting of humility, gentleness, patience, bearing with other

Christians and maintaining our spiritual unity. This is God's will and should be prayed for by individual believers as well as congregations of Christians. Have you prayed lately for these guaranteed legitimate requests? These are attributes God desires to develop in his children in response to believing prayer.

One more prayer instruction is found in Ephesians 6:10-20:

> *Finally, be strong in the Lord and in the strength of his might. Put on the whole armor of God, that you may be able to stand against the schemes of the devil. For we do not wrestle against flesh and blood, but against the rulers, against the authorities, against the cosmic powers over this present darkness, against the spiritual forces of evil in the heavenly places. Therefore take up the whole armor of God, that you may be able to withstand in the evil day, and having done all, to stand firm. Stand therefore, having fastened on the belt of truth, and having put on the breastplate of righteousness, and, as shoes for your feet, having put on the readiness given by the gospel of peace. In all circumstances take up the shield of faith, with which you can extinguish all the flaming darts of the evil one; and take the helmet of salvation, and the sword of the Spirit, which is the word of God, praying at all times in the Spirit, with all prayer and supplication. To that end keep alert with all perseverance, making supplication for all the saints, and also for me, that words may be given to me in opening my mouth boldly to proclaim the mystery of the gospel, for which I am an ambassador in chains, that I may declare it boldly, as I ought to speak.*

This well-known passage describes our spiritual battle and our weapons in this battle, but how does it relate to prayer? Having the "armor of God" is God's will. Thus, pray this armor into place according to his will. We are exhorted to "Pray at all times in the Spirit," meaning guided and directed by the Spirit rather than praying fleshly prayers based on our will rather than God's.

Next Paul instructs us to pray with supplication for the saints. Other believers need our prayers to be sustained through their spiritual battles. It is God's will that we pray for them, not neglecting this responsibility. Finally Paul prays for a bold proclamation of the Gospel. We can't pray that for Paul 2000 years after his death, but we can pray it for those today who proclaim the message of salvation in Christ, not to mention praying for our own boldness.

CONCLUSION

There's no better way of learning to pray than following the biblical examples, of which there are many. The prayers of Hannah, Daniel and Paul demonstrate praise, confession and petition according to the will of God in a most dramatic way. Pray like they prayed and get answers like they received. Will you let their examples transform your prayer life? But now we turn to perhaps the most famous example of prayer.

APPLICATION & IMPLEMENTATION

1. Take Hannah's prayer of praise in I Samuel 2 and offer it to God in prayer.

2. Alter Daniel's prayer for his people to fit your own nation and situation.

3. Petition God for the characteristics Paul prayed to develop in Ephesian believers. Note the difference you experience praying these petitions as compared to your usual prayers.

THIS CHAPTER IN A NUTSHELL

1. The Bible is full of great examples of prayer that show us the way.

2. Hannah's prayers reflect honest appeal to the mercy of God in affliction and exalted praise.

3. Daniel's prayer demonstrates praying from a biblical basis,

plus focusing on confession of sin and appeal to God's reputation.

4. Paul's prayers for the growth and maturity of believers are appropriate petitions for any Christian.

FOOTNOTES:

1. Keller, Timothy, *Prayer: Experiencing Awe and Intimacy with God*, (New York: Penguin Books, 2014), p. 80.

Chapter 12

Radical Model – The Lord's Prayer

I used to think the Lord's Prayer was a short prayer; but as I live longer, and see more of life, I begin to believe there is no such thing as getting through it. If a man, in praying that prayer, were to be stopped by every word until he had thoroughly prayed it, it would take him a lifetime. – Henry Ward Beecher

Most of us have memorized it. It is, without doubt, the most familiar prayer in the world. Tens of millions recite it every Sunday in liturgical churches. Yet it is also the most abused and misused. Martin Luther described the Lord's Prayer as:

> *. . . the greatest martyr on earth because it was used so frequently without thought and feeling, without reverence and faith.*

Untold numbers of books have scraped the Milky Way examining the Lord's Prayer. Rather than add to their volumes, my goal is simply to show how it serves as a model for prayer, illustrating the principles we're discussing in this book. From the Sermon on the Mount, here is the actual prayer:

> *Our Father in heaven, hallowed be your name. Your kingdom come, your will be done, on earth as it is in heaven. Give us this day our daily bread, and forgive us our debts, as we also have forgiven our debtors. And lead us not into temptation, but deliver us from evil.* (Matt. 6:9b-13)

Let's examine the prayer from the point-of-view of its ironies:

Irony #1 – Misnomer

Though called the "Lord's Prayer" for centuries, it really should not be called the *Lord's* Prayer, since Jesus never prayed this prayer. In fact Jesus, being sinless, *could not* pray this prayer asking for forgiveness. It might better be called "The Disciple's Prayer," since it was given to teach them how to pray, I prefer to call it what Jesus intended it to be – The Model Prayer.

Irony #2 – Not a Ritual

While untold numbers pray these exact words repeatedly, Jesus never intended us to pray this as a ritual of magic words. He said, "Pray then *like* this" (Matthew 6:9a). Thus, it is an outline of elements of appropriate prayer – a model. Pray *like* this, but not necessarily these exact words. Of course there's nothing inherently sinful with praying these exact words if you really believe them and have contemplated their meaning.

Irony #3 – Rebuke to Meaningless Repetition

We need to ask ourselves, "Why did Jesus give this prayer model?" He offered this as a rebuke:

> *But when you pray, go into your room and shut the door and pray to your Father who is in secret. And your Father who sees in secret will reward you. "And when you pray, do not heap up empty phrases as the Gentiles do, for they think that they will be heard for their many words. Do not be like them, for your Father knows what you need before you ask him. Pray then like this:* (Matt. 6:7-9a)

"Pray like this" was a rebuke to vain repetition in prayer. Yet today people recite the Lord's Prayer as vain repetition of ritual words, devoid of their full meaning. Let's look at the elements of the prayer model.

OUR FATHER

How is it that we are instructed to pray to "our" Father instead of just "my" Father? Certainly this prayer is not restricted to group praying, but may be prayed by a lone individual. I think this is a relational issue in which we proclaim our unity with other believers sharing the same Father. We see this union of our Lord with the disciples:

> *I am ascending to my Father and your Father, to my God and your God.* (John 20:17b)

Jesus is not only our Savior and Lord, but also our elder Brother in this relationship. We are all in this together as a family.

Have you considered how outrageous it is to call God "Father?" The Pharisees certainly reacted to that language:

> *This was why the Jews were seeking all the more to kill him, because not only was he breaking the Sabbath, but he was even calling God his own Father, making himself equal with God.* (John 5:18)

Christianity alone calls God "Father." We take this incredible truth for granted, perhaps not considering how this amazing fact came to be. First, we have God as our Father by redemption, having been bought out of the slave market of sin:

> *. . . for you were bought with a price. So glorify God in your body.* (I Corinthians 6:20)

> *But now you have been set free from sin and have become slaves of God.* (Romans 6:22a)

Secondly, God is our Father by adoption. We are not *natural* children to God, since Adam's fall and resulting spiritual death terminated that relationship. We could only be brought back into God's family by adoption:

> *. . . he predestined us for adoption through Jesus Christ, according to the purpose of his will.* (Ephesians 1:5)

> *But when the fullness of time had come, God sent forth his Son, born of woman, born under the law, to redeem those who were under the law, so that we might receive adoption as sons. And because you are sons, God has sent the Spirit of his Son into our hearts crying, "Abba, Father!"* (Galatians 4:4-6)

As important and godly as adopting children is in our culture, the adoption referred to in the New Testament is a practice even more amazing – Roman adoption. In this adoption typically a wealthy, childless man would adopt a young man to be his heir and continue his family lineage, taking his name. All claims to his natural father were terminated. All debts were cancelled by the new father. The adoptee literally became a new person. While a *natural* child could be disowned in the Roman system, an *adopted* child could never be disowned. It was a permanent, secure relationship. In my quiet time recently I started praying and meditating from this model and couldn't get past "Our Father," as I pondered how amazing it was that he chose me for adoption as his child. I again realized the truth of Henry Ward Beecher's quote, noted earlier, that it would take a lifetime to thoroughly pray this prayer.

Contrary to some cults, there is no universal fatherhood of God that all human beings can claim. Though we were all *created* by God, creation doesn't equate with fatherhood. I can "create" a bookshelf in my workshop, but that doesn't make it my "child." You can only be a child by birth, by redemption or by adoption. We actually have all three: we were born again by the Spirit, redeemed by Christ's blood sacrifice and adopted into his family.

Actually the Bible makes this even clearer by noting there are *two* fatherhoods: The Fatherhood of God through redemption and adoption, and the fatherhood of the Devil, by natural birth into Adam's race:

> *You are of your father the Devil . . .* (John 8.44)

We start out as members of the Devil's family, but by grace and mercy are adopted into God's family when we come to faith in Christ.

To be able to call God our "Father," transforms the way we think about bringing petitions to him. Ezekiel Hopkins notes:

> *If the heart of an earthly parent, whose tender mercies are cruelties in comparison with god, does not allow his children to be defeated in their requests, how much more will God who is love and goodness itself . . .*

He will not allow his children to return ashamed when they beg of him those things which are most agreeable to his will and to their wants . . . Ask for your good, and you will receive it.[1]

IN HEAVEN

What is the significance of noting that God is in heaven as we pray? By praying "in heaven," recognizing his transcendence, we acknowledge God's authority. When it comes to prayer, don't you want to appeal to the highest authority? Back to our legal courtroom analogy, if possible you would desire your case to be heard before the highest court – the Supreme Court – knowing that it wouldn't be reversed later. The fact that God is "in heaven" gives confidence to our prayers.

YOUR KINGDOM COME

So what is the kingdom of God? Consider these references by Jesus Christ:

> Kingdom is "at hand" (Matthew 3:2, 4:17)
> Kingdom is "in the midst of you" (Luke 17:20-21)
> Kingdom "has come upon you" (Matthew 12:28)
> You will "see the Son of Man coming in his kingdom (Matthew 16:28-17:8)

The kingdom is anticipated throughout the Old Testament and proclaimed as having commenced in the New Testament.

A "kingdom" requires two things: a king and an established rule by that king. Obviously we have the King, but what about his rule? Parables such as The Mustard Seed and The Leaven teach us about the expansion of the kingdom of God from its small beginnings. God's kingdom rule has been growing since the earthly ministry of Jesus and the Apostles. The final verse of the Book of Acts notes:

> *. . . proclaiming the kingdom of God and teaching about the Lord Jesus Christ with all boldness and without hindrance.* (Acts 28:31)

Paul describes the fulfillment of the kingdom this way:

> *But each in his own order: Christ the firstfruits, then at his coming those who belong to Christ. Then comes the end, when he delivers the kingdom to God the Father after destroying every rule and every authority and power. For he must reign until he has put all his enemies under his feet.* (I Corinthians 15:23-25)

We read the final fulfillment of the kingdom of God in Revelation:

> *Then the seventh angel blew his trumpet, and there were loud voices in heaven, saying, "The kingdom of the world has become the kingdom of our Lord and of his Christ, and he shall reign forever and ever."* (Rev 11:15)

So why pray for the kingdom to come? The ultimate objective of God is to rule without dispute. What was lost by Adam is being restored in the second Adam, Jesus Christ. As noted in I Corinthians, Christ is reigning until defeating all his enemies . . . and we're part of that as his "army." It is a long battle, with many ups and downs over two thousand years, but it is moving to a conclusion in God's time. When we pray for his kingdom to be realized, we are reaffirming our commitment and allegiance to his cause . . . and that means surrendering our own "cause," as noted previously by Alan Redpath:

> *Before we can pray, "Lord, Thy Kingdom come," we must be willing to pray, "My Kingdom go."*

YOUR WILL BE DONE

We talked of God's decrees and will in earlier chapters. The question again arises, "Why pray if God's will is guaranteed to happen?" As previously discussed, we recognize that our prayers are also decreed and through prayer we are privileged to participate in the fulfillment of God's purposes. Nevertheless, perhaps the bigger issue concerns not how prayer changes "things," but how it changes us. In genuine prayer we encounter God, and you cannot encounter God without being transformed.

God's kingdom and will are connected. The "kingdom" concerns the overall rule God is establishing throughout history culminating in the Second Coming of Christ, while his "will" is more of the details. This phrase from the model prayer thus moves from general to specific.

ON EARTH AS IT IS IN HEAVEN

God's will is done perfectly in heaven, while sin caused it not to be done on earth. The rebellion of the children of Adam is being conquered, though the brief period of our individual lives may not see the progress. Preaching the Gospel ushers God's kingdom in on a personal level, which in turn affects institutions and society as a whole as demonstrated in past spiritual awakenings.

DAILY BREAD

The only petition for personal, temporal needs in the Lord's Prayer asks for daily bread. Everything else in the prayer outline concerns God, his glory, his purposes and being in right relationship with him. But God, who is good and kind and compassionate, knows well our daily needs. Later in Matthew 6, Jesus amplifies this by saying:

> *Therefore do not be anxious, saying, 'What shall we eat?' or 'What shall we drink?' or 'What shall we wear?' For the Gentiles seek after all these things, and your heavenly Father knows that you need them all.* (Matt 6:31-32)

This additional text makes clear that "daily bread" concerns more than food, but rather includes all our basic needs – food, clothing and presumably shelter.

Note that the prayer is for *daily* needs – not weekly, monthly or yearly needs. God desires that we trust him every day rather than just occasionally. Contrast this admonition with the Parable of the Rich Fool in Luke 12:13-21 who wanted to provide for himself for years to come. He was a fool because he wanted to secure his future provision through his own effort. He was a fool because he had no knowledge of what the future would bring – namely his own death that very night.

God not only knows we need these basic necessities of life, but also knows we tend toward anxiety concerning these needs. He knows our weakness. Thus, we are instructed to pray about this, surrendering daily our anxiety of basic needs. While God provides for us physically, he desires to refocus our attention on the greater objective:

> *But seek first the kingdom of God and his righteousness, and all these things will be added to you.* (Matt 6:33)

Seek God's kingdom as your first objective and you needn't worry about provision of basic needs.

FORGIVE OUR DEBT OF SIN

If you've been around church very much, you know some churches recite the Lord's Prayer saying "debts," while others say "trespasses." The text actually says "debts," from the Greek word *opheimlema* which means "something owed" or "debt." The idea is that sin is a spiritual debt owed to God. Other scriptures use this same language, such as the Parable of the Unforgiving Servant in Matthew 18:23-27. The servant was forgiven a monumental debt by his master only to refuse to forgive a small debt owed him by another servant. The parable describes the "settling of accounts" in the kingdom of God. Jesus then applies the parable to God's requirement that we forgive others "from our heart," obviously referring to those who sin against you.

Romans 6:23 similarly likens sin to indebtedness:

> *For the wages of sin is death, but the free gift of God is eternal life in Christ Jesus our Lord.*

What a contrast! Sin earns a wage – a wage of death, while God's life is a gift of free grace. Calvin amplifies our understanding of the terminology:

> *In Matthew, sins are called debts, because they expose us to condemnation at the tribunal of God, and make us debtors; nay more,*

> *they alienate us entirely from God, so that there is no hope of obtaining peace and favor except by pardon. And so is fulfilled what Paul tells us, that "all have sinned, and come short of the glory of God." (Romans 3:23)*

Likewise Matthew Henry notes:

> *Our sins are our debts; there is a debt of duty, which, as creatures, we owe to our Creator; we do not pray to be discharged from that, but, upon the non-payment of that there arises a debt of punishment; in default of obedience to the will of God, we become obnoxious to the wrath of God; and for not observing the precept of the law, we stand obliged to the penalty. A debtor is liable to process, so are we: a malefactor is a debtor to the law, so are we.*

AS WE FORGIVE OUR DEBTORS

To best understand this part of the petition we need to continue with the Parable of the Unforgiving Servant. In his case forgiveness was withdrawn because he didn't forgive. The question arises then as to how such forgiveness *not* works-based? Do we receive forgiveness *because* we have forgiven others? The issue is not really about works, but about grace. The grace of forgiveness by God motivates a response of forgiveness toward others. To do otherwise is inconsistent with the meaning of grace. Matthew Henry comments:

> *This is not a plea of merit, but a plea of grace. Note, those that come to God for the forgiveness of their sins against him, must make conscience of forgiving those who have offended them, else they curse themselves when they say the Lord's Prayer.*

To forgive others demonstrates that we have indeed received God's grace, while to not forgive others brings that into question.

LEAD US NOT INTO TEMPTATION

This petition, first of all, recognizes our constant threat of temptation, as Jesus expressed elsewhere:

> *Watch and pray that you may not enter into temptation. The spirit indeed is willing, but the flesh is weak.* (Matthew 26:4; parallel passages in Mark 14:38 and Luke 22.40)

However, there is also recognition that God will limit how much we are tempted:

> *Therefore let anyone who thinks he stands take heed lest he fall. No temptation has overtaken you that is not common to man. God is faithful, and he will not let you be tempted beyond your ability, but with the temptation he will also provide the way of escape that you may be able to endure it.* (I Corinthians 10:12-13)

While the threat of temptation recognizes our sin nature, the limit acknowledges the goodness and mercy of God. He doesn't keep us from all temptation, but he does keep us from that which we cannot handle. Here we petition God to prevent us from sin.

DELIVER US FROM EVIL

This petition concerns deliverance from sin when petition has failed. "Deliver" is the Greek word *rhuomai*, which is translated "rescue." God is still concerned when we need rescue, having failed to prevent sin. Imagine how pitiful our state would be if God did not both protect *and* rescue us from sin. That should be motivation to offer this petition.

Many commentators translate this "from the evil one," namely Satan, rather than just "from evil." While we need deliverance from doing evil *things*, we specifically need deliverance from the evil *one*, the enemy of our souls. Even as one without a sin nature, our Lord nevertheless endured multiple temptations from Satan, whom Peter exhorts us to:

> *Be sober-minded; be watchful. Your adversary the devil prowls around like a roaring lion, seeking someone to devour. Resist him* . . . (I Peter 5:8-9a)

MODEL PRAYER PROGRESSISON

Let's summarize the progression of the Model Prayer:

- We acknowledge our relationship with God as his adopted child
- We praise God for his holiness
- We petition for the fulfillment of his rule on earth
- We petition for his will to subdue a rebel race
- We petition for the daily needs of his children
- We pray for forgiveness
- We pray for protection and rescue from sin

We have been given a perfect model of prayer. It reveals God's will, which in turn allows us to align our prayers with that will. While this is called "The Lord's Prayer," the real Lord's Prayer is the one Jesus himself prayed for us. That's next.

APPLICATION & IMPLEMENTATION

1. Pray using the Lord's Prayer as an outline rather than saying the words by rote. Expand on each petition to fit your current situation.

2. As you pray, using the Lord's Prayer as an outline, pause to meditate on the meaning of each line to deepen your understanding of its concepts.

THIS CHAPTER IN A NUTSHELL

1. The Lord's Prayer would be better called "The Disciple's Prayer" or "The Model Prayer."

2. This prayer outline was given as a rebuke to meaningless repetition in prayer – the very way it is typically used today.

3. Addressing God as "Father" was a radical concept.

4. The prayer outline focuses on the fulfillment of God's purposes.

5. The only petition for personal, temporal needs is for "daily bread."

6. The prayer requests both prevention and rescue from sin.

FOOTNOTES:

1. Ezekiel Hopkins, Works, 1:53-63, as quoted from Richard Rushing, Editor, Voices from the Past, (Carlisle, PA, The Banner of Truth Trust, 2009), p. 136.

Chapter 13

Radical Relationship – The *Real* Lord's Prayer

We cannot ask in behalf of Christ what Christ would not ask Himself if He were praying. – A. B. Simpson

If the "Lord's Prayer" isn't really the *Lord's*, what is the real Lord's Prayer? We find the prayer that Jesus actually prayed in John 17 – sometimes called the "High Priestly Prayer." In this prayer we learn the valuable truth of how Jesus prayed and what he prayed for. Following his example will further transform our prayers.

GLORIFYING GOD & FULFILLING HIS PURPOSE

Not surprisingly, this prayer begins with praise and giving glory to God:

> *When Jesus had spoken these words, he lifted up his eyes to heaven, and said, "Father, the hour has come; glorify your Son that the Son may glorify you, since you have given him authority over all flesh, to give eternal life to all whom you have given him. And this is eternal life, that they know you the only true God, and Jesus Christ whom you have sent. I glorified you on earth, having accomplished the work that you gave me to do. And now, Father, glorify me in your own presence with the glory that I had with you before the world existed." I have manifested your name to the people whom you gave me out of the world. Yours they were, and you gave them to me, and they have kept your word. Now they know that everything that you have given me is from you. For I have given them the words that you gave me, and they have received them and have come to know in truth that I came from you; and they have believed that you sent me.* (John 17:1-8)

To "glorify" is to exalt or praise in the context of worship. We catch a glimpse into the activity of the Trinity in this passage and see a mutual glorification society. More significantly for us, later in the prayer we are invited into that circle of praise.

Much of this glorification centers on Christ fulfilling the purposes of the Father. Christ says he has the authority to give eternal life to those whom the Father gave him. Do you realize that we – the elect of God from before the foundation of the world (Ephesians 1:4) – were a present from the Father to the Son? I almost get dizzy thinking about it! The Father chose not to save any of the fallen angels from Lucifer's rebellion and yet chose to save a multitude from every nation, tribe and tongue to give to the Son that he might redeem them through his incarnation and death in payment of their sin. This is the inner workings of the Trinity. I can only say with Charles Wesley, "Amazing love; how can it be!" A couple other verses amplify the Father's gift to the Son:

> *All that the Father gives me will come to me, and whoever comes to me I will never cast out.* (John 6:37)

> *... who saved us and called us to a holy calling, not because of our works but because of his own purpose and grace, which he gave us in Christ Jesus before the ages began ...* (II Tim 1:9)

The fulfilled purpose of Christ proclaimed in his prayer is that:

- We would know the Father
- We would know the Son
- We would be called out of the world to salvation

No wonder that soon after this Jesus would proclaim on the cross, "It is finished." What was finished? The purpose for which he came. The question for us is simple:

> *Is fulfilling God's purposes the focus of my prayer life?*

WHAT JESUS PRAYED FOR US

Jesus is praying for you and me. To say that is a sobering thought to put it mildly! We continue reading in John 17:

> *I am praying for them. I am not praying for the world but for those whom you have given me, for they are yours. All mine are yours, and yours are mine, and I am glorified in them. And I am no longer in the world, but they are in the world, and I am coming to you. Holy Father, keep them in your name, which you have given me, that they may be one, even as we are one. While I was with them, I kept them in your name, which you have given me. I have guarded them, and not one of them has been lost except the son of destruction, that the Scripture might be fulfilled. But now I am coming to you, and these things I speak in the world, that they may have my joy fulfilled in themselves. I have given them your word, and the world has hated them because they are not of the world, just as I am not of the world. I do not ask that you take them out of the world, but that you keep them from the evil one. They are not of the world, just as I am not of the world. Sanctify them in the truth; your word is truth. As you sent me into the world, so I have sent them into the world. And for their sake I consecrate myself, that they also may be sanctified in truth. "I do not ask for these only, but also for those who will believe in me through their word, that they may all be one, just as you, Father, are in me, and I in you, that they also may be in us, so that the world may believe that you have sent me. The glory that you have given me I have given to them, that they may be one even as we are one, I in them and you in me, that they may become perfectly one, so that the world may know that you sent me and loved them even as you loved me. Father, I desire that they also, whom you have given me, may be with me where I am, to see my glory that you have given me because you loved me before the foundation of the world. O righteous Father, even though the world does not know you, I know you, and these know that you have sent me. I made known to them your name, and I will continue to make it known, that the love with which you have loved me may be in them, and I in them."* (John 17:9-26)

Looking at this part of the prayer, here is my basic premise:

What Jesus prayed for us, we can confidently pray for ourselves, knowing it is God's will.

So let's take a look at what he prayed for. First, he prayed for believers, not the world. Jesus, unlike us, had no prayer for the unbelieving world. He wasn't praying for unbelievers to become believers, as discussed in our earlier chapter on petition. That issue was settled in eternity past. His focus was on those whom the Father gave him, namely, his sheep, as discussed earlier in John's gospel:

> *I am the good shepherd. I know my own and my own know me, just as the Father knows me and I know the Father; and I lay down my life for the sheep. And I have other sheep that are not of this fold. I must bring them also, and they will listen to my voice. So there will be one flock, one shepherd.* (John 10:14-16)

The "other sheep" of course are us – the Gentiles.

PRESERVATION OF THEIR FAITH

Jesus is leaving, but the disciples are staying. The mission of redemption of the fallen world is not yet complete. Humanly speaking, it depends on them – or more accurately, if depends on God working through them. Jesus prays five petitions in this regard:

- **Keep them in your name** – To be "in God's name" is to be relationally connected. He prays that their identity would be in God as functioning members of his family carrying out his mission.

Keep them one as we are one – To understand what this unity looks like, we must first consider what the oneness of the Trinity looks like. How are the Father and Son one exactly? They are not identical but have different roles in the Godhead. They are one in their commitment to each other. They are also one in purpose. All Christians are not the same. All Christians don't go to the same local church. All Christians don't have the same doctrinal beliefs on non-essential matters. Though we're different in many ways, we at least should have oneness in our commitment to other believers and to our mission.

- **Keep them in Christ's joy** – Isn't it interesting that one of the main petitions for us is that we would experience the joy of Christ? Joy is the fortress for believers under affliction in a hostile, fallen world carrying out Christ's mission.

- **Keep them in the world but protected** – As disciples of Christ we are in the world on purpose – on God's purpose. We are here to fulfill Christ's mission as the Second Adam to restore what was lost by the first Adam. While joy is our inner protection from discouragement in a world rebellious to God, externally God protects us from the Evil One – Satan. Jesus prays that we would be kept from the influence of Satan and his host as we fulfill God's purposes.

- **Sanctify them in truth** – To sanctify literally means to set apart for special use – to be holy. Jesus prays that we would be set apart in the truth of God. Identification with God's truth is the key to sanctification. That should be our distinctive in this world.

THOSE WHO WILL BELIEVE

Perhaps the most exciting part of this prayer is that we're included today – "those who will believe in me through their word" (17:20). This isn't just a prayer for those original eleven disciples, but rather for all believers in all time. Jesus prays for you and me to be unified as the Father and Son are unified. This repeated concept is clearly foremost in the mind of the Lord because it is so essential to fulfilling his redemptive mission – "that the world may believe." Our relational, as well as mission oneness, speak to the unbelieving world.

Jesus' great desire is to spend eternity with his children:

> *Father, I desire that they also, whom you have given me, may be with me where I am, to see my glory that you have given me because you loved me before the foundation of the world.*

What a tender love he expresses about those for whom he has died. He desires that we see him in his glorified state that existed from before the foundation of the world. I believe this expresses his desire that we see that Jesus is who he said he is – that our faith is not in vain.

Jesus states that he has made the Father's name known *and* that he will continue to make it known. This again speaks of Christ's intercessory role at the right hand of the Father. He prays that the love relationship of the Father and Son would be experienced by believers. He desires that we be drawn into the circle of the Trinity.

7 THINGS WE MAY PRAY

So what prayer petitions may we appropriate from this passage, knowing they are God's will for us as believers? Christ prays for seven things to happen in us that we can confidently pray as well:

1. Keep me walking with God
2. Give me the joy of relationship with Christ
3. Keep me from satanic defeat
4. Sanctify me
5. Give me unity with other believers
6. Build in me an anticipation of eternity with Christ
7. Allow me to experience God's great love for me

Unlike a lot of our prayer requests, these prayer requests will transform our lives – as Kierkegaard said, they will "change the nature of the one who prays."

APPLICATION & IMPLEMENTATION

1. Meditate on John 17, visualizing yourself as an eavesdropper to this conversation within the Trinity. What new insights come to you?

2. Pray the petitions for yourself that Jesus prayed for you in this prayer. Observe your confidence in these petitions being fulfilled.

THIS CHAPTER IN A NUTSHELL

1. John 17 is the real "Lord's Prayer" and shows how Jesus prayed and what he prayed for.

2. After praising God, this prayer emphasizes fulfilling God's purposes.

3. Jesus' prayer concern is for believers, not for the unbelieving world.

4. He prays for continuing faithfulness in our relationship with God, the experience of his joy and protection from being spiritually drawn away.

5. What Jesus prayed for us we can legitimately pray for ourselves.

Closing Thoughts

Prayer may not change things for you, but it for sure changes you for things.
— Samuel M. Shoemaker

The objective of this book is simple – to lead you into the practice of biblical prayer. I believe God would shift our prayer focus from primarily praying for things to praying to know God better. In an intimate relationship with him all our needs are met, though we must acknowledge that our greatest need is God himself and knowing him better. He would have us simply spend time with him through prayer rather than merely recite a Christmas list of our desires.

The simplest advice I could give on prayer can be summed up in five points:

- **Listen more**
- **Praise more**
- **Meditate more**
- **Petition less**
- **Find a biblical basis for your petitions**

No matter how mature we become in our prayer life, our prayers will invariably fall short, for we are of a fallen race. Our best attempts, which we should strive for, will still fall short. Yet, like a safety net, we are covered in those short-comings with Paul's encouragement in Romans 8:26-27:

> *Likewise the Spirit helps us in our weakness. For we do not know what to pray for as we ought, but the Spirit himself intercedes for us with groanings too deep for words. And he who searches hearts knows what is the mind of the Spirit, because the Spirit intercedes for the saints according to the will of God.*

This is not an exhortation to resigning ourselves to a mediocre prayer life any more than God's grace is a license to sin. As the Apostle would tell us, "May it never be!" Nevertheless we can be encouraged that God, in his goodness and mercy, knows our weakness and does compensate for it through the Holy Spirit's intercession. While our prayers will never be perfect, they can mature and they most definitely can radically transform our relationship with God.

About the Author

After growing up in the Midwest, Monte Kline came to the Pacific Northwest in pursuit of a college education in earth science and to enjoy the region's scenic beauty. However, coming to know Christ his sophomore year changed his plans, redirecting him after graduation into several years of college campus Christian ministry. During that time he developed a serious cancer condition that was ultimately resolved with a natural medicine approach. This experience launched him into a career of speaking, writing books and presenting health and nutrition from a biblical perspective, including *Eat, Drink & Be Ready*, *The Junk Food Withdrawal Manual*, *Vitamin Manual for the Confused*, *The Sick & Tired Manual*, *Body, Mind & Health* and *Health Dare: 8 Reasons to Try Natural Healing*. After completing a graduate degree in Nutrition & Wholistic Health Sciences, Monte went into practice as a Clinical Nutritionist in 1984. He currently directs a virtual health practice remotely testing clients from around the world.

Monte also has a ministry focus on growing intimacy with God through Personal Retreats, as detailed in his book, *Face to Face: Meeting God in the Quiet Places* and his ministry website: www.christianpersonalretreat.com.

Monte has served in teaching and pulpit capacities in several local churches and also writes the Historic Faith theology blog (www.historicfaith.wordpress.com). For several years he has focused on personal study and teaching classes on the biblical design for prayer as reflected in this book.

Monte, along with his wife Nancy, live near Tucson, Arizona.

Appendix A – Emotional & Spiritual Health

Encounter God through Personal Retreats

Dealing with the "missing ingredients" of *physical health* is one thing, but what about your emotional and spiritual health? How do you bring healing to those areas? My suggestion: Have an **encounter with God** – what I call a **Personal Retreat**.

Has God spoken to you lately? Imagine a whole new way of meeting with God that would transform your Christian life. What if you could create special times alone with God for illumination, direction on decisions, and just the sheer enjoyment of being in His presence . . . like nothing you ever experienced before? What if you could come "face to face" with God? My book, ***Face to Face: Meeting God in the Quiet Places*** provides the blueprint. Following the pattern of Abraham, Elijah, Paul, and Jesus, ***Face to Face*** shows the way to create those life-changing encounters. You will discover:

A way to meet with God and hear his voice

Keys to escaping the "noise" and busyness of life

An alternative to "Christmas list" praying

How to "capture" your spiritual transformation

How to encounter God through Personal Retreats

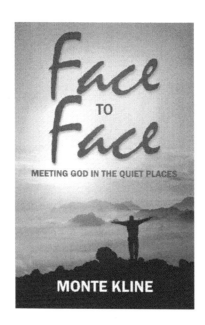

What others say . . .

> ***Face to Face*** *lays out a game plan for a deeper and more meaningful relationship with Christ.* – Tom Flick, Motivational Speaker and former NFL quarterback
>
> *Only you and Him. It stands to reason you need some quality time* ***Face to Face.*** – Stu Weber, Author of Tender Warrior

Order at this link: http://www.amazon.com/dp/B00M1ZBIU8

Appendix B

Discover Health in Body, Mind and Spirit

The Bible recognizes that we are body, mind and spirit, but how does that relate to our everyday health? How do we discover our physical, emotional and spiritual ingredients of health? Simply by going back to God's design. Our Creator is in the business of producing wholeness in body, mind and spirit. We are "healthy" when we are "whole." Our health problems therefore stem from the "holes" in our "wholeness." What physical ingredients of health are you missing? What emotional ingredients? What spiritual ingredients? BODY, MIND & HEALTH probes these questions providing practical answers through nutrition, detoxification, exercise, emotional stress release, and spiritual renewal.

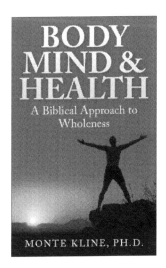

Chapters:

Your Health Checklist
God-Made Food
Water that Refreshes
Cleansing that Purifies

By the Sweat of Your Brow
Let the Sun Shine
Sleep that Satisfies
Healthy Attitudes
Capturing the Present Moment
Resolving Emotional Stress
Spiritual Roadblocks to Health
Defeating Spiritual Strongholds
Total Health at the Cross
Living in God's Sovereignty

> *Excellent book. I learned a lot from reading it. The author has really done his research. One of the key things I learned from this book is that healing comes from many sources such as emotional, spiritual, and mental, not just the physical aspect, which tends to be the one aspect that most people tend to focus on. Very enlightening. I highly recommend it*
> -- Shawn Clark

Order at this link: http://www.amazon.com/dp/B00M9TFQKE

Made in the USA
Lexington, KY
03 January 2018